THE
SMALL
GUIDE TO
ANXIETY

THE SMALL GUIDE TO ANXIETY

GARY SMALL, MD, AND GIGI VORGAN

Humanix Books

www.humanixbooks.com

Humanix Books

The Small Guide to Anxiety
Copyright © 2019 by Humanix Books
All rights reserved

Humanix Books, P.O. Box 20989, West Palm Beach, FL 33416, USA
www.humanixbooks.com | info@humanixbooks.com

Library of Congress Cataloging-in-Publication Data is available
upon request.

Interior Design: Scribe Inc.

Humanix Books is a division of Humanix Publishing, LLC. Its
trademark, consisting of the words "Humanix" is registered in the
Patent and Trademark Office and in other countries.

Disclaimer: The information presented in this book is not specific
medical advice for any individual and should not substitute medical
advice from a health professional. If you have (or think you may have)
a medical problem, speak to your doctor or a health professional
immediately about your risk and possible treatments. Do not engage
in any care or treatment without consulting a medical professional.

ISBN: 978-1-63006-089-3 (Trade Paper)
ISBN: 978-1-63006-090-9 (E-book)

Printed in the United States of America
10   9   8   7   6   5   4   3   2   1

Contents

Acknowledgments

WE ARE GRATEFUL TO the many volunteers and patients who participated in the research studies that inspired this book as well as the talented investigators who performed the studies. Thank you to our colleagues, friends, and family members who provided their encouragement and input, including our daughter Rachel and our son Harrison. Thank you to Diana Jacobs for the drawings of the brain. We also appreciate the support and guidance from our longtime agent and friend, Sandra Dijkstra, her entire team, as well as Mary Glenn at Humanix Books and Chris Ruddy at Newsmax Media.

Gary Small, MD, and Gigi Vorgan

Note: Many stories and examples contained in this book are composite accounts based on the experiences of several individuals and do not represent any one person or group of people. Similarities to any one person or persons are coincidental and unintentional. Readers may wish to talk with their doctor before starting any exercise or diet program.

Prologue

ALMOST EVERY ONE OF us has been or will be affected by anxiety during our lifetimes. Anxiety is a universal feeling often experienced as a state of unease over upcoming events or uncertain future outcomes. It could be a response to an immediate threat or to something imagined that might happen in the future. Whether the anxiety trigger is in the present or an anticipated future, many events and situations contribute to our anxiety.

During World War II, the threat of fascism dominating the free world was a major source of anxiety. During the Cold War, people worried about the possibility of a nuclear disaster. Today, we fret about terrorism, privacy, environmental issues, political upheaval, unstable economies, and more. Social media platforms such as Facebook, Instagram, and Snapchat provide a conduit for sharing our experiences with others; however, they often contribute to a persistent form of anxiety and peer pressure—a need to be better, happier, richer, and more successful than the others on our friends list.

Anxiety has surpassed depression as the most common reason that young adults and teens seek counseling. A recent national survey of college students indicated that in 2015, more than 60 percent of undergraduates felt overwhelmed by anxiety.

Studies show that when anxiety, stress, or worry drag out or become chronic, the resulting physical changes can suppress the immune system. Such suppression will weaken the body's defenses against infection and contribute to coronary artery disease and even heart attacks.

This book will help you distinguish normal anxiety responses from more extreme forms of distress known as anxiety disorders, which disrupt our ability to get things done. It will not only help you better understand what contributes to your anxiety; it will also help you determine whether your discomfort in a given situation is reasonable or perhaps out of proportion to the circumstances.

In the chapters ahead, you will learn several do-it-yourself techniques to lower your anxiety symptoms and how to determine whether you could benefit from professional help. Taking action to reduce your anxiety will not only improve your well-being and brain health; it will also reduce your risk of physical illnesses and help you live longer and better.

CHAPTER 1

What Is Anxiety?

*Don't worry about the world
coming to an end today; it's already
tomorrow in Australia.*
—Charles Schulz

LINDA HEARD THE CLOCK ticking as the second hand slowly lurched forward. She tried to slow her breathing—in, out, in, out—but she just couldn't get enough air. Her heart pounded like it might burst out of her chest, and she could feel her sweat soaking through her dress. "Okay," she told herself, "it's just a job interview—not so scary."

Avoiding eye contact with the other applicants in the waiting room, Linda stared at her résumé, but her eyes couldn't focus. "I'll never get this job," she thought. "Why did I come? No way do I have as much experience as these other girls."

She felt a sudden urge to urinate just as the receptionist called out, "Linda Fuller?"

Linda stood up quickly but got dizzy and had to sit back down.

"Are you Linda?"

She tried to answer, but her mouth was too dry.

"Well, you're next," the receptionist said impatiently. "Down the hall on the right."

Linda got up more slowly this time and started walking down the hall, but she felt her throat closing up and she froze in fear. "If I don't get out of here," she thought, "I'm going to die." She felt a wave of nausea coming up and bolted for the exit.

*   *   *

Anxiety is a normal human emotion that everyone feels from time to time, and it's very common to feel a bit anxious before a job interview. In Linda's case, however, her anxiety escalated so much that she had a panic attack, and that is relatively rare.

Most people experience anxiety as a state of unease or apprehension over an upcoming event or an uncertain outcome. It can manifest itself in various ways, and although it is usually an unpleasant feeling, most of us can either channel our anxiety into actions that dissipate the concern or accept that we can't control the outcome. People who suffer from panic attacks and other anxiety disorders often misinterpret nervousness or stress as actual physical danger that must be avoided at all costs. And although many people think of fear and anxiety as the same thing, they are actually very different.

Fear is generally an emotional response to a real and imminent threat. It is characterized by a fight-or-flight response, where the person feeling fear either confronts the source or flees from it, and the fear usually dissipates as soon as the threat is gone. Anxiety, on the other hand, is worry and anticipation of a possible threat or conflict in the future and can linger or become chronic.

Today, we face few situations that call for a fight-or-flight response. Most of our day-in, day-out worries are more mundane, like whether traffic will make us late for an appointment or whether the boss will be in a bad mood today. In recent years, however, a growing sense of impending danger from terrorism, environmental concerns, political upheaval, and disease epidemics has crept into our consciousness and left many feeling persistently apprehensive. Instead of focusing chiefly on achieving their best, many people now worry more about preventing the worst. Although this type of ongoing, low-level anxiety can be a bothersome distraction, most of us don't allow these worries to erode our overall sense of well-being.

When we say we feel anxious, we are usually describing feelings of nervousness, worry, excessive concern, or apprehension. But some people, such as Linda at the job interview, experience anxiety so intensely that it causes physical and emotional symptoms that disrupt their lives. These people suffer from an anxiety disorder—their worries and fears have gotten so severe that they are unable to live normally.

The physical and emotional symptoms that characterize anxiety disorders can become so excruciating that left untreated, the patient's life can become severely restricted and intolerable. Germophobes can become too paranoid to dine out, fear of panic attacks can keep people from going out in public, and anxiety-induced chest pains can be mistaken for life-threatening heart attacks.

Linda's inability to deal with her anxiety made her physically ill and sabotaged her job interview. As her anticipation of rejection overwhelmed her, it manifested itself in acute physical symptoms. When her anxiety escalated, her thinking became distorted to the point that she felt she was going to die. People with extreme anxiety disorders can often feel like they are in a life-or-death situation when they are not.

Linda is among millions of people of all ages and backgrounds that struggle with anxiety disorders and often suffer unnecessarily—usually because they assume that nothing can be done to relieve their symptoms. This is simply not true. Anxiety disorders are highly treatable: several successful medical interventions, lifestyle strategies, and alternative therapies are available, yet currently, only about one out of every three sufferers receives proper treatment.

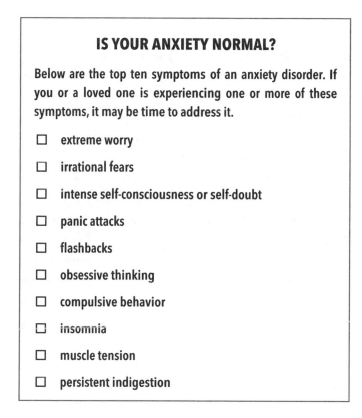

IS YOUR ANXIETY NORMAL?

Below are the top ten symptoms of an anxiety disorder. If you or a loved one is experiencing one or more of these symptoms, it may be time to address it.

☐ extreme worry

☐ irrational fears

☐ intense self-consciousness or self-doubt

☐ panic attacks

☐ flashbacks

☐ obsessive thinking

☐ compulsive behavior

☐ insomnia

☐ muscle tension

☐ persistent indigestion

THE ANXIETY EPIDEMIC

Anxiety disorders are the most frequent of all psychiatric diseases. As the problems in our world seem to worsen every year, there has been a corresponding increase in the prevalence of anxiety disorders. In 1980, only 4 percent of Americans were thought to be suffering from anxiety, but today, that number has risen to 18 percent. Approximately one in five

Americans age eighteen or older, or about forty million people, suffer from them. In comparison, only one in ten of us suffers from a mood disorder like depression, the second most common type of psychiatric problem.

The economic burden that anxiety places on society is considerable, totaling $42 billion each year, or a third of our entire mental health bill. About half of these health care expenses go to the assessment and treatment of medical symptoms and consequences of anxiety.

If you have an anxiety disorder, you are five times more likely to go to the doctor or six times more likely to be hospitalized for a psychiatric condition than someone without an anxiety disorder. Severe symptoms of anxiety can lead to other conditions like ulcers and substance abuse, which take their own physical, emotional, and financial toll on sufferers. Chronic anxiety disorders also disrupt marriages and other relationships and have adverse effects on a person's education, job, and social life.

WHY AM I SO ANXIOUS?

Sometimes we feel anxiety and are not sure why. No single cause can explain the many forms of anxiety, but past experiences and genetic predispositions

---

DID YOU KNOW?

Many young adults and teenagers become overwhelmed by anxiety, which has surpassed depression as the most likely reason they seek counseling. According to the American College Health Association's 2016 survey of students, 62 percent of undergraduates reported feeling overcome by anxiety in 2015, a significant increase from 50 percent in 2011.

---

will determine each individual's risk of developing a disorder. These factors have an impact on our brain chemistry, personality style, and tolerance for stress, which ultimately determine who will develop normal, mild anxiety symptoms or a full-blown disorder.

If one of your parents was high strung or suffered from an anxiety disorder, your own risk increases. For the average person, genetic inheritance accounts for about 30 to 40 percent of the risk.

In addition to passing on their DNA or genetic material to us, our parents' behavior impacts our ability to cope and adapt to fearful situations, beginning at a very young age. Whether our parents modeled healthy responses to stress or taught us their own anxious reactions will shape our own coping ability and temperament. A person who has a personality that is rigid, volatile, pessimistic, or insecure will likely have greater difficulty with anxiety than a more resilient, optimistic, and self-confident individual.

Physical illnesses and medication side effects can also lead to anxiety symptoms. For instance, patients with diabetes who take too much insulin will often experience an acute anxiety attack from a sudden drop in blood sugar.

Sometimes an anxiety disorder can be confused for a physical illness. In studies of patients who go to the emergency room complaining of chest pain and fearing cardiac disease, more than 40 percent of them are suffering from a panic disorder or panic attack rather than a heart problem. Also, heavy coffee drinkers are at risk of experiencing heart palpitations and other anxiety symptoms due to excess caffeine consumption.

If you are a woman, you are 60 percent more likely to suffer from an anxiety disorder than if you are a man. Your age will influence your risk as well. One of the upsides of getting older is that we tend to experience less anxiety. Young people live with greater peer pressure and increased worry about the future: building a career, finding a partner, having a family, and facing the unknown. As years pass, we gain more perspective on these concerns and they don't seem as urgent or important. We also learn better ways to cope with our anxiety. It's not surprising that the prevalence of anxiety in people ages eighteen to

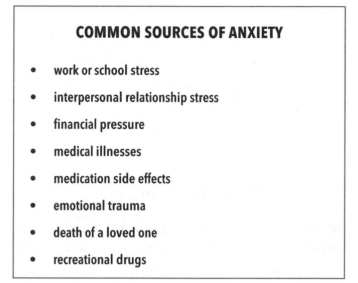

COMMON SOURCES OF ANXIETY

- work or school stress
- interpersonal relationship stress
- financial pressure
- medical illnesses
- medication side effects
- emotional trauma
- death of a loved one
- recreational drugs

fifty-nine is about 30 percent but only 15 percent in people ages sixty and older.

It's also true that as we get older, we experience different forms of anxiety. A majority of older people develop chronic physical illnesses, which can trigger considerable anxiety. As people age, they also worry more about their memory, and patients with Alzheimer's disease and other dementias commonly suffer symptoms of anxiety.

DID YOU KNOW?

Anxiety can make the world stink. When we become more anxious, our olfactory systems–the brain's neural circuits that control our sense of smell–are heightened, and we are better able to distinguish a neutral odor from something that smells bad.

THE ANXIOUS BRAIN

Several brain areas are involved in controlling our anxiety responses. The amygdala, a tiny region that resides beneath the temples of the forehead, serves to regulate our feelings of anxiety and fear. The amygdala interacts with another deeper brain region, the nucleus accumbens, and when this neural network becomes overstimulated, we experience anxiety and fear.

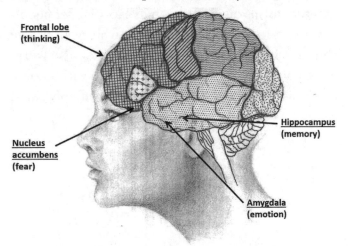

Anxious people often have hypersensitive amygdalae. When facing unfamiliar situations, they may experience exaggerated stress that results in physical symptoms (rapid heart rate, increased blood pressure) and amplified emotional responses.

The hippocampus, which resides near the amygdala, converts these exaggerated experiences into long-term memories. Over time, these memories can heighten one's sensitivity to other similar situations that are benign and set off the amygdala's inflated anxiety response unnecessarily.

Another brain region activated by anxiety is the frontal lobe, also called the "thinking brain." This part of the brain processes uncomfortable emotions and attempts to put them into perspective. Sometimes heightened anxiety can overload the frontal lobe's capacity to regulate emotional responses.

Chronic or even intermittent stress can cause wear and tear on the brain regions that control our responses. For example, research indicates that the hippocampus is actually smaller in people who were abused as children or were in military combat.

Regardless of the form of anxiety, when a person perceives danger, his or her brain triggers the body's sympathetic nervous system, which responds by releasing adrenaline, cortisol, and other stress hormones into the blood. This then sets off the fight-or-flight response.

As anxiety escalates, it can lead to an imbalance of specific brain messengers—called neurotransmitters—such as gamma-aminobutyric acid (GABA), dopamine, and epinephrine. Various anxiety-related genes have been discovered that influence how our brain's chemical messengers (e.g., adrenaline and serotonin) and hormones (e.g., cortisol) can alter our emotional states. For example, serotonin is essential to our well-being, and when it declines, it can lead to anxiety and even depression. In conditions such as panic disorder, the amount of the stress hormone cortisol in the brain rises, increasing feelings of fear and dread.

DID YOU KNOW?

Recent research has demonstrated a link between verbal intelligence and the severity of worry and rumination. Investigators at SUNY Medical Center in New York also reported that people with anxiety disorders have higher IQs. These studies don't necessarily prove that anxiety makes you smarter because it may be that smarter people are more aware of things that may stimulate nervousness.

TECHNOLOGY ANXIETY

Advances in technology in recent years have made our lives more efficient and created simple and immediate ways to communicate with others. And although the emergence of the internet and twenty-four-hour news cycles helps keep us informed and connected, receiving a constant flow of information can serve to continually remind us of things that make us anxious. Thanks to our smartphones and other handheld devices, we receive moment-to-moment updates on current events that can often be stressful or even terrifying.

Social media outlets like Facebook, Instagram, and Snapchat have become a dominant presence in our lives and provide a conduit for sharing our experiences with others. For many anxious people, however, they contribute to an unrelenting form of peer pressure—a need to be better, happier, richer, and more successful than the others on our friends list.

These sites are distracting as well. Technology expert Linda Stone described the concept "continuous partial attention," in which people constantly keep tabs on several things at once while never truly focusing on much of anything. When we bombard our brains with data, information overload can lead to anxiety.

TRY THIS

The next time you feel anxiety bubbling up, give this simple mindfulness exercise a try:

- Sit in a comfortable chair, place your feet flat on the floor, and allow them to point slightly outward.

- Rest your hands on your thighs with your palms facing up and close your eyes.

- Take eight deep, slow breaths in through your nose, exhaling through your mouth.

- Feel your body relaxing as your mind grows peaceful.

- Continue inhaling and exhaling slowly for another minute or two, then open your eyes.

PSYCHOLOGICAL VERSUS PHYSICAL ANXIETY

Most of us think of anxiety as an emotion, but anxiety symptoms and disorders can have prominent physical components. Your first clue that you are feeling anxious may be your racing pulse, pounding heart, or a sensation that you can't catch your breath. Some people suffer an upset stomach or sweaty palms.

We all experience situational stress and worry, but these are usually transient states that get resolved. People who experience chronic stress or extreme worry for an extended time may be living in a persistent fight-or-flight state, which continually triggers the body to release increased amounts of the stress hormone cortisol. Persistently high cortisol levels can lead to a variety of physical symptoms ranging from difficulty swallowing to muscle aches, shortness of breath, and sweating. Cortisol also increases levels of blood sugar and fats, which are meant to fuel the body to take quick action under conditions of acute stress. Unfortunately, when stress or worry drag out or become chronic, the resulting physical changes can suppress and weaken the immune system, leading to infection and illness.

This overlap of physical and psychological symptoms of anxiety can be confusing to patients and doctors, especially when physical symptoms of anxiety are mistaken for a medical illness. A rapid heart rate caused by an oncoming panic attack may be construed as a life-threatening heart arrhythmia.

Other times a physical illness may be causing psychological symptoms. Poor concentration or irritability could be due to decreased oxygen to the brain from pneumonia or another infection. Some patients suffer from both an anxiety disorder and physical illness at the same time, which makes it even more challenging to figure out the true underlying source of anxiety symptoms.

PSYCHOLOGICAL SYMPTOMS OF ANXIETY

apprehension

compulsive thoughts

dread

edginess

fear or terror

irritability

memory loss

nervousness

obsessive thinking

panic

phobia

poor concentration

worry or rumination

PHYSICAL SYMPTOMS OF ANXIETY

dizziness

dry mouth

chest pain

fatigue

headache

rapid heartbeat, skipped beats

muscle tension / aches

nausea / upset stomach / loose stool

numbness/tingling

shortness of breath

sweating

trembling/twitching

trouble swallowing

THE DANGERS OF UNTREATED ANXIETY

There are a variety of reasons that one out of every three people suffering from an anxiety disorder never receives adequate treatment. Anxiety patients generally avoid stressful situations, and most patients find it stressful to see the doctor about their symptoms. A shortage of mental health professionals, difficulty diagnosing anxiety disorders, denial about the severity of symptoms, and the perception that nothing can be done to help also contribute to undertreatment. Many people play down the impact of mental symptoms on their health, but research has shown that untreated anxiety disorders can diminish a person's ability to function even more than many medical conditions such arthritis, diabetes, and heart disease.

Clearly, not getting help can be dangerous to your health and well-being. Untreated anxiety disorders increase the risk of depression and even suicide. As anxiety-driven physical symptoms and illnesses worsen, the patient's health care costs tend to rise—often due to frequent emergency room visits when panic attacks and physical symptoms overwhelm them.

Relationships suffer as well. Patients frequently feel misunderstood and become isolated from family and friends. Anxiety disorders can disrupt or ruin a patient's professional life too. The symptoms distract the patient from completing tasks, increase their number of sick days, and can lead to significant financial losses.

The good news is that anxiety disorders can be effectively treated. The first step toward treatment is for patients to admit that their symptoms are disrupting their lives and to seek help. Whether a person is suffering from a full-blown anxiety disorder or less severe symptoms, determining the type of anxiety disorder will help clarify the most effective treatment for the condition.

ANXIETY SYMPTOMS CAN TRIGGER SUICIDAL THOUGHTS

Although most of us think of depression as the most likely trigger for suicidal thinking, people suffering from untreated anxiety disorders can also develop thoughts of suicide and act upon those thoughts. The recent tragic suicides of designer Kate Spade and celebrity chef Anthony Bourdain has brought greater awareness to the growing problem of suicide.

In the United States, suicide rates have risen by 25 percent during the last two decades. In 2016, there were almost forty-five thousand suicides in the United States, which is twice the number of deaths compared with homicides. Major risk factors for suicide include chronic depression, history of alcohol or substance abuse, access to lethal weapons, impulsivity, feelings of hopelessness, social isolation, and barriers to mental health treatment. Although suicidal individuals may not ask for help, they often do want it.

One of the greatest myths about suicide is that discussing the topic will plant the idea in someone's mind. Stay alert to some of the warning signs of suicidal risk:

- feelings of hopelessness and emptiness
- statements about wanting to die
- online searches on suicidal methods
- feelings of guilt or shame
- expressions of extreme physical or emotional pain
- excessive use of alcohol or drugs
- mood swings
- withdrawing from family and friends
- dramatic changes in behavior or weight
- a change in eating or sleeping habits
- expressions of rage
- risk-taking behavior (e.g., reckless driving)
- giving away possessions

Anyone having thoughts of suicide should consult with a mental health professional. Help is also available through the National Suicide Prevention Lifeline at 1-800-273-TALK (8255).

TAMING ANXIETY

Regardless of the type of anxiety symptoms or disorder you or your loved one may be experiencing, effective treatments and self-help strategies are available. Interventions vary depending on the specific disorder. For example, patients with panic disorder often

COMMON TYPES OF ANXIETY DISORDERS

- *Generalized Anxiety Disorder*: persistent and excessive worry about everyday things that continues for months or longer with various symptoms, including fatigue, poor concentration, insomnia, muscle tension, and restlessness

- *Panic Disorder*: recurrent and unexpected sudden episodes of intense fear accompanied by rapid heartbeat, skipped beats, sweating, trembling, shortness of breath, and feelings of impending doom

- *Social Anxiety Disorder*: fear of social or performance situations where feelings of rejection or embarrassment are anticipated

- *Phobic Disorder*: irrational fear or anxiety about and avoidance of a specific object or situation

- *Agoraphobia*: excessive fear or anxiety about one or more situations, such as public transportation, open spaces, enclosed spaces, crowds, or being outside the home alone, that may lead one to become housebound

- *Obsessive-Compulsive Disorder*: chronic, uncontrollable, and persistent thoughts (obsessions) and behaviors (compulsions) that the individual feels compelled to repeat over and over

benefit from both antidepressants and desensitization therapy. The antidepressants reduce the acute symptoms of panic, and the desensitization therapy helps patients overcome the phobias they may have developed to avoid the attacks. Many approaches, however, such as meditation, physical exercise, and psychotherapy can be useful for taming nearly all forms of anxiety.

REFRAMING NERVOUSNESS INTO EXCITEMENT

In order to minimize stress and calm your nerves about an upcoming challenge, try to reframe your feelings of worry into feelings of excitement. For instance, if you are nervously fretting over a presentation you'll be giving at work, flip those feelings of nervousness to feelings of excitement over how well it will go because you are prepared. Studies show that this kind of reframing is much more effective in reducing anxiety symptoms than trying to suppress your feelings.

Psychotherapy. Different forms of talk therapy can reduce anxiety symptoms and contribute to remission of disorders. By talking regularly with a mental health professional (psychiatrist, psychologist, social worker, or other counselor), patients are able to better understand their behaviors, emotions, and ideas that contribute to their symptoms and learn how to make positive changes. Cognitive behavioral therapy helps people identify and challenge negative patterns of thought about themselves and the world in order to alter unwanted behavior patterns. Supportive psychotherapy helps a person explore troubling issues and provides emotional support, while desensitization therapy exposes patients to their anxiety-provoking fears for brief periods in a supportive environment to increase their tolerance to those fears.

Medications. Antianxiety medicines, such as Ativan, Xanax, and other benzodiazepines, can reduce the acute psychological and physical symptoms of anxiety. Although they are usually the first medication choice for treating depression, antidepressant medications are also effective in treating many of the symptoms of obsessive-compulsive disorder and panic disorder.

Lifestyle strategies. Adopting and maintaining healthy behaviors can reduce anxiety symptoms. Regular physical exercise and a balanced diet not only improve mood and reduce symptoms; they also benefit memory and cognitive abilities. Relaxation methods and mindfulness techniques, such as meditation, hypnosis, yoga, tai chi, deep breathing, and other forms will lower stress levels and anxiety symptoms and even rewire neural circuits in the brain.

ANXIETY AND DIET

A study published in the *American Journal of Psychiatry* demonstrated an association between higher anxiety symptoms and a typical "Western" diet consisting of fried foods, refined grains, sugary products, and beer. Study subjects who consumed more vegetables, fruit, meat, fish, and whole grains were less likely to suffer from anxiety.

Other therapies. Various supplements (e.g., kava, valerian, St. John's wort) and innovative treatments (eye movement desensitization and reprocessing [EMDR], neurofeedback, transmagnetic stimulation [TMS]) have been used to relieve anxiety. Some of these interventions show promise and are still under scientific investigation, while others have not yet been shown to be more effective than placebo but are still used by many people.

CHAPTER 2

Do-It-Yourself Strategies for Reducing Anxiety

One advantage of talking to yourself is that you know at least somebody's listening.

—Franklin P. Jones

WHEN ANY OF US feels anxious, our natural response is to find a way to relieve the discomfort. It could be as simple as avoiding a perceived danger or talking things over with a friend to gain some perspective.

Whether you only experience anxiety from time to time or have an anxiety disorder, you've probably tried some do-it-yourself strategies to calm down. Perhaps you went to the gym for a workout, tried to meditate, or breathed into a bag. These well-known approaches often have calming effects, but there are other strategies that may reduce your symptoms even more.

A lot of us feel anxious because we take on too many tasks. Becoming overcommitted is easy, but learning to delegate can be harder. Most people don't know that simply *asking* others for assistance can reduce anxiety significantly.

TRY THIS

In the evening or before bed, make a list of appointments and to-do items for the next day. Prioritize your list according to what you absolutely must do yourself, what you can ask others to do, and what can be delayed until another time. This process can go a long way to relieve anxiety.

Various forms of talk therapy can help people gain a better perspective on their worries, but a conversation with an empathic friend can also be a great stress reducer. Be honest about what's bothering you—your friend may give you a new viewpoint or at least let you vent.

Learning to recognize what triggers your anxiety is essential to devising ways to dissipate your symptoms. For instance, if you identify that a certain individual brings up anxiety symptoms for you, try to distance yourself from that person and minimize contact. Certain environments can also trigger people to feel anxious or overwhelmed.

*   *   *

Elaine never liked shopping. Perhaps it was because she got lost in a huge department store when she was a child, but even supermarkets overwhelmed her, and she felt anxious every time she needed groceries. Eventually, Elaine was able to develop a do-it-yourself remedy that helped—she began by shopping at the same market every time. She also made a shopping list beforehand and remained focused on finding only those items while in the store. She began to feel calmer when shopping because she had a clear objective and didn't have to make a bunch of choices or new decisions.

*   *   *

Once an anxiety trigger is identified, it becomes easier to address. Below is a list of common triggers and some do-it-yourself remedies. See if any apply to you so you can begin to devise your own ways to lessen the impact of your triggers.

ANXIETY TRIGGERS AND WHAT YOU CAN DO ABOUT THEM

Trigger	Solution
Doctor's appointment	Make a list of questions and medicines to discuss.
Stock market ups and downs	Divest your portfolio into lower risk investments.
Dreaded family reunion	Keep it as brief as possible and avoid confrontation.
Public speaking	Rehearse and do relaxation exercises.

Having a negative attitude can breed anxiety, so working to keep a positive outlook is another helpful strategy for soothing your nerves. Learning optimism is not as hard as it may seem. Some people are born seeing the cup half full. They appreciate the good things in their lives and don't dwell on the bad. But even if you are the cup-half-empty type—perhaps you ruminate on what bad thing might happen next—turning that attitude around and reducing your anxiety is not that difficult. The process often involves letting go of guilt and breaking the habit of always expecting the worst outcome in any situation.

TRY THIS

- Think of a situation that makes you anxious–perhaps a disagreement with a friend or worry over being late for work.

- In your mind, play out your anticipated negative outcome of this situation, such as possibly losing that friendship, getting fired, and so on.

- Begin to concentrate on your breathing. Take a few deep, slow inhales and exhales. Continue to focus on your breath coming in and going out, and feel yourself relaxing mentally and physically.

- Consider the anxiety-provoking situation and try to see the bigger picture: even if your boss gets upset over your tardiness, you are not likely to lose your job over it, and with all the good times you and your friend have spent together, it is unlikely that one spat will unravel your relationship.

Using this approach allows you to step back, relax, and put your worries into perspective so you can recover a positive attitude more quickly.

The following self-help approaches have all been shown to be effective in reducing stress. The best way to discover which method or methods work best for you is to try a few of them.

RELAXATION TECHNIQUES

When I notice I'm feeling anxious, whatever the reason, the first thing I try to do is relax myself so that I can think calmly and clearly. This isn't always as easy as it sounds, but using the tried and true techniques below has helped me and many of my patients.

Progressive Muscle Relaxation

Anxious individuals often have taut muscles, which leads to aches and pains and worsens psychological tension. This may be why one of the most popular and easy relaxation techniques is *progressive muscle relaxation*. It involves scanning your body from the top of your head down to your feet and systematically releasing any tension you are holding in your muscles. Controlled studies have shown that progressive muscle relaxation is more effective than a placebo medication treatment in reducing symptoms of a number of anxiety disorders, including generalized anxiety disorder, panic disorder, and social phobia.

Meditation

This popular practice involves sitting or lying comfortably and focusing attention on a phrase, breath, sound, or object. It's normal for the mind to wander, but with practice, meditators become able to recognize when that happens and to gently guide their

TRY THIS

- Get comfortable in a chair or on a mat.

- Take a deep breath, then let it out and close your eyes.

- Focus your attention on your forehead. Notice any tension there and consciously allow those forehead muscles to relax.

- Now move your attention to the muscles around your eyes and release the tension there. Next, let the sense of relaxation spread down to your jaw and neck.

- Continue to systematically relax every muscle group in your body as you move down to your shoulders, arms, torso, and so on until you reach your toes.

- Take a last deep inhale and exhale, then open your eyes.

attention back to the breathing, phrase, or object they were focusing on.

Meditation reduces negative thinking and helps us relax, thus lowering stress and anxiety. The practice has been shown to improve mood and memory while altering brain neural circuits. Many studies have shown that meditation increases the size of the brain's grey matter, the outer rim where brain cells reside. Larger grey matter volume is associated with a lower risk of memory and other age-related cognitive declines. Meditation also increases overall brain wave function and activates the thinking brain (frontal lobe) and emotional brain (amygdala).

TAKE A RELAXING MEDITATION BREAK

For a quick mindfulness boost, take a few minutes to try this exercise:

- Sit in a comfortable chair and place your feet flat on the floor in a comfortable position.

- Rest your hands gently on your thighs, and close your eyes.

- Begin taking slow breaths in and out through your nose. Focus on the coolness of the air as it enters your nostrils and the warmth of the air as you slowly exhale.

- If your mind wanders to random thoughts about errands you have to do, calls you have to make, and so on, gently guide it back to the feeling in your nostrils as the air moves in and out.

- Feel your body relax as your mind grows peaceful.

- Continue for another minute or two, then open your eyes.

Several controlled studies indicate that meditation reduces symptoms in generalized anxiety and panic disorders. People who meditate enjoy improved

EXAMPLES OF MEDITATION TECHNIQUES

- *Guided Meditation*: Involves meditating with the guidance of an instructor who makes suggestions as to what to focus attention on, such as images, sounds, and breathing. Guided meditation apps can be downloaded to your smartphone or tablet and can be helpful for beginners and those with more experience with meditation.

- *Affirmative Meditation*: Uses positive affirmations regarding health, mood, confidence, or other areas to encourage a particular way of feeling or thinking.

- *Mindfulness Meditation*: Focuses less on making positive changes and more on becoming aware of and staying in the present from moment to moment. It helps one observe mental flow without judgment.

- *Transcendental Meditation*: Trains the mind to become calm, silent, and "empty." Usually involves repetition of a mantra, word, or phrase.

- *Progressive Muscle Relaxation*: Entails monitoring of tension in a particular muscle or body area, relaxing that region, and then progressively spreading that relaxation throughout the body.

- *Self-Hypnosis*: Focuses attention on certain messages to improve particular aspects of thinking, believing, or perception, allowing the practitioner to enter a relaxed state. It is often used to control habits and behaviors as well as to reduce pain.

cognitive abilities, and MRI research indicates positive alterations in brain neural circuitry from just ten minutes of daily meditation.

Many forms of meditation offer these types of beneficial effects. When starting out, it can be helpful to try various styles to see which one works best for you.

Autogenic Training

Autogenic training involves retraining the mind to reduce stress and calm the body through simple mental exercises. This approach helps the body respond to mental or verbal commands that one tells oneself in order to control one's heartbeat, breathing, temperature, blood pressure, pain, and more. Although many people find it helpful for reducing anxiety, there is limited research on its effectiveness. Autogenic training is similar to biofeedback in that they both focus on the autonomic nervous system, which regulates body functions not controlled by the conscious mind. However, autogenic training requires the use of biofeedback devices to objectively monitor these functions.

Journaling

Another way to gain perspective on your worries and lower your anxiety levels is to keep a diary or journal. Research has shown that psychotherapy patients who maintain a personal journal feel less anxiety than those who do not. Journaling has also been shown to reduce worrying in those with generalized anxiety disorder.

Keeping a log or diary of our activities and emotional reactions over time allows us to reflect on our experiences and feelings and gain insight on them. Writing about our feelings, just as talking about them, can in itself reduce stress levels.

If this is something new for you, start by finding a quiet time and comfortable place where you won't be interrupted and begin writing about whatever comes to mind. Spelling and grammar don't count—just date your entry and let the thoughts and feelings flow.

GET A GOOD NIGHT'S SLEEP

Anxiety at bedtime can definitely keep us up at night. Insomnia—which refers to trouble falling asleep, problems staying asleep, waking up too early, or getting up and not feeling refreshed—is very often anxiety related. Anxious people with sleep problems tend to become even more anxious due to their lack of sleep.

Insomnia and sleep deprivation are known to increase the risk of developing an anxiety disorder. Sleep problems can also aggravate physical conditions, such as hypertension, diabetes, or obesity, which can further threaten brain health and increase the risk of cognitive and mood changes.

TIPS FOR IMPROVING SLEEP

- Avoid daytime naps.

- Pick a regular bedtime and stick to it.

- Don't consume caffeine in the evening.

- Break the habit of lying in bed and engaging in nonsleep activities (e.g., eating, surfing the net, watching TV, talking on the phone).

- Get daily exercise but not too close to bedtime.

- Listen to calming music and use a timer to shut it off automatically if possible.

- Meditate to drift off–consider using a meditation app for sleep.

- Try this systematic approach that promotes better sleep habits:
    - Get into bed the same time each evening.
    - Meditate or use another relaxation method to settle down.
    - If you are not asleep in twenty minutes, get out of bed and do something else–read a book, listen to music.
    - When you begin to feel tired, go back to bed and try to fall asleep.
    - If you're still awake after twenty minutes, get out of bed and do something else again.

○   **Keep repeating this routine throughout the night.**

○   **Make sure you don't nap the next day, and repeat the above steps the next night.**

○   **By the third night, it should be easier for you to fall asleep on the first attempt.**

Self-help techniques can not only fight insomnia and improve restful sleep; they can also reduce symptoms of anxiety. Many do-it-yourself strategies like meditation, deep breathing exercises, and progressive muscle relaxation can help people get to sleep at night as well as fall back to sleep if they have awakened.

A patient once complained to me that he would read in bed every night until he felt tired. However, when he reached over to turn off the light and tried to settle back down, all that movement just woke him up again. He finally figured out a solution—after shutting off the light, he would get into a comfortable position, lie perfectly still, and then focus on his breathing. This was his way of meditating to sleep.

Various illnesses, such as depression and heart disease, and medication side effects can disrupt sleep. If you think you have a sleep disorder, it's important to discuss your symptoms with your doctor. Talking therapies can be helpful, particularly cognitive behavior therapy for insomnia, which teaches people to identify and alter the behaviors that disrupt their sleep. Several online cognitive behavior therapy programs for insomnia are available (e.g., SHUTi, sleepio) so you can learn these techniques yourself.

Depending on the cause of the sleep problem, the doctor may or may not prescribe a medication. Depressed patients may sleep better when they take a sedating antidepressant medicine, but beware of other common types of sleeping pills like Ambien or Lunesta because they can become habit forming. Also, some over-the-counter sleep aids can cause memory side effects, particularly in older people who already notice mild forgetfulness. I always recommend trying self-help methods to induce restful sleep before using sedatives.

PHYSICAL ACTIVITY

Cardiovascular conditioning boosts memory, mood, and energy while reducing brain-damaging neural inflammation. The mood-lifting effects of aerobic conditioning have been shown to help patients suffering from anxiety and depression.

It's not necessary to become a triathlete or gym rat to appreciate the calming effects of aerobic workouts. Just twenty minutes a day of brisk walking has been shown to provide significant brain advantages and stress reduction.

Some people like to work out on their own, while others prefer fitness classes or competitive sports. Exercising with others introduces an important social element that provides additional mental health benefits. It's important to find an exercise regimen you enjoy because that will help you stick with it and gain the most benefits. Keep in mind that beginners should start low and go slow to avoid injury and gradually build stamina.

Yoga is a popular mind-body exercise that involves postures, breathing, and meditative elements, and research on the benefits of yoga for anxiety disorders is encouraging. The slow, deliberate meditative postures and movements of tai chi have been shown to improve mood, memory, and physical stamina while altering brain neural circuitry for the better.

Dancing combines an aerobic workout with the cognitive challenge of keeping track of your movements and steps. Brain scans of experienced dancers demonstrate strengthened neural circuits in regions involved in motor control, balance, and social interaction compared to scans of beginners. Don't forget that household chores can provide a fairly good workout too. Raking leaves and making beds for thirty minutes can knock off one hundred or more calories.

APPROXIMATE CALORIES BURNED
DURING THIRTY-MINUTE ACTIVITIES

Calories counts listed are averages for a 155-pound individual but will vary according to a person's body weight and rigor.

Activities	Calories
Sleeping, watching TV	25
Cooking	95
Bowling, dancing, volleyball, Frisbee, lifting weights	110
Golf or food shopping (using cart)	130
Horseback riding, tai chi, stretching, yoga, water aerobics, raking	150
Gardening, mowing lawn, badminton, walking (15 min./mile)	170
Snorkeling, softball, dancing (ballroom, square)	190
Golf (carrying clubs)	205
Swimming, power walking	230
Racquetball, tennis, soccer, cycling	260
Basketball, cycling (12 mph), football, hockey, running (5 mph)	300
Elliptical machine	335

If you don't mind the stress of a larger credit card bill, shopping at the mall can give you a workout while boosting your neural circuits. You will benefit from both the aerobic exercise you get walking briskly between stores as well as the neural stimulation that comes from searching through items for the right sizes and colors. Shopping with a friend adds an important social interaction element that can reduce stress, stimulate the brain, and make exercising more fun.

DID YOU KNOW?

- Eating fast food, sweets, and processed food can make you more anxious.

- A twenty-minute brisk exercise session can reduce your anxiety almost immediately.

- Anxious individuals are more sensitive to people encroaching on the immediate area surrounding them—that is, their *personal space*.

Many people like to go to gyms that offer indoor aerobic options and strength training with weights. Both aerobic conditioning and strength training get our hearts pumping more oxygen and nutrients into our cells, which boosts physical and mental energy, stabilizes mood, and helps reduce anxiety. If you're pressed for time, try interval training, which involves periods of intense exertion alternated with periods of rest or lighter exertion. Recent research indicates that you receive the same health benefits from this pattern of exercise in one fourth the time needed for endurance training.

Another mental benefit of cardiovascular conditioning is the euphoria we experience as the feel-good hormones, endorphins, get released into our systems. These mood-stabilizing hormones can allay anxiety and depression.

PHYSICAL ACTIVITIES FOR REDUCING ANXIETY

- *Aerobic Conditioning*: climbing, cycling, using the elliptical, working on household chores, interval training, jogging, running, swimming, running on a treadmill, walking, practicing yoga

- *Strength Training*: free weights, Pilates, resistance bands, yoga, weight lifting machines

- *Competitive Sports*: badminton, baseball, football, Ping-Pong, basketball, racquetball, soccer, tennis

- *Dancing*

- *Other Activities*: shopping, performing household chores, and gardening

FOOD FOR MOOD

Most of us enjoy eating a variety of foods, and we know that healthy meals are essential to fortify our bodies. But what and how much we eat can also impact our mood. Dining can be one of the greatest pleasures in life, and sharing meals with others is a good way to socialize, reduce stress, and improve overall wellbeing.

Eating fruits, whole grains, and vegetables that provide important vitamins and minerals is associated with a lower risk of depression. Also, foods high in omega-3 fats like fish, nuts, and flaxseed improve mood. Eating carbohydrates in moderation can have a calming effect in part because they increase the amount of the mood-enhancing brain chemical serotonin. Experts speculate that low brain serotonin levels may be linked to "carb cravings." The amino acid tryptophan contained in some protein-rich foods like chicken, turkey, and tuna can also increase serotonin in the brain.

Many people who get stressed out or anxious turn to food for comfort. Whether it's a grilled cheese sandwich, slice of chocolate cake, or bowl of sugary cereal, eating comfort foods can bring temporary anxiety symptom relief. But when eaten in excess, these foods lose their calming effects and can lead to health problems associated with being overweight or obese. Scientists have found that people who

THE GLYCEMIC INDEX

The glycemic index (GI) ranks carbohydrates from zero to one hundred depending on their complexity and how rapidly they are digested and absorbed as sugar (glucose) into the blood. For better brain health and less anxiety, it's best to emphasize some of the following low GI carbs and avoid the high GI carbs in our diets:

GI Rating	Foods
< 40	Apple, apricots (dried), bean sprouts, cashews, fettuccine, grapefruit, lentils, lima beans, nonfat yogurt, peanuts, prunes, skim milk, soybeans, wheat tortilla
40–54	All-bran cereal, baked beans, corn tortilla, cooked carrots, grapes, oatmeal, orange, peach, quinoa, spaghetti, whole-grain bread, unsweetened apple juice
55–75	Bananas, brown rice, Cream of Wheat cereal, ice cream, natural Muesli cereal, oat-bran cereal, pineapple, potato chips, white pita bread, whole-wheat bread
71–84	Bagels, Cheerios, Cocoa Puffs, Corn Flakes, French fries, jelly beans, pretzels, puffed wheat cereal, rice cakes, soda crackers, Total cereal, vanilla wafers
≥ 85	Baked potato, dried dates, white baguettes, instant mashed potatoes, instant rice

regularly consume fast foods, processed foods, and sweets are generally more anxious than those who eat natural foods, such as poultry, milk, seeds, and nuts.

Eating a Mediterranean-style diet that includes fruits, vegetables, lean proteins, and omega-3 fats from fish, nuts, or flaxseed provides anti-inflammatory properties that protect both our brains and our bodies from heightened inflammation associated with aging. Simply limiting our intake of refined sugars and pro-cessed foods has been shown to reduce inflammation and lower stress levels and anxiety. It also decreases our risk of age-related diseases like diabetes and Alzheimer's.

Complex carbohydrates such as whole grains take longer to digest so they help stabilize blood sugar levels and provide a steadier supply of serotonin to the brain. By contrast, high-glycemic index carbs will spike blood sugar levels and lead to subsequent blood sugar dives that trigger hypoglycemia—a potentially dangerous mental and physical state that causes anx-iety symptoms including nervousness, sweating, diz-ziness, and a pounding or racing heart.

Caffeine is the world's most widely consumed stim-ulant and is present not only in coffee and tea but also in cola, chocolate, and many other foods. Too much caffeine will make people feel nervous and restless and worsen symptoms of anxiety, so it makes sense to limit caffeine consumption to promote calmness.

Any anxious person attempting to reduce their caffeine intake should go about it gradually since rapid caffeine withdrawal can cause headaches, fatigue, moodiness, and irritability.

Many of us are familiar with that satisfied but somewhat lethargic state we feel after a big Thanksgiving dinner. One explanation is a possible relaxation effect from the tryptophan-rich turkey meal. Tryptophan is an amino acid that may have antianxiety effects because it changes into serotonin when it enters the brain. Research on pumpkin seeds, another tryptophan-rich food, indicates that eating them can reduce symptoms of social phobia.

TECHNOLOGY AND ANXIETY

In today's technology-laden world, it seems like new innovations, gadgets, programs, or apps come out almost every day. These tech wonders are often designed to simplify our lives, streamline our work, give us more free time, and help us communicate more efficiently. While many people find these advances helpful for reducing stress, others experience increased anxiety with each new innovation.

Many people enjoy social media platforms like Facebook, Instagram, and Snapchat, which allow them to stay in touch with each other and share their experiences and photographs. However, these sites can leave some individuals feeling bad about their own, less-exciting lives and increase their emotional isolation. Such isolation can bring on feelings of loneliness and self-doubt, which often cause anxiety or worsen existing concerns. It's important to pick and choose the technology tools that help reduce your stress rather than increase it.

Numerous websites and apps are available to help people who suffer from anxiety, and the Anxiety and Depression Association of America and other organizations provide reviews of many of them. These programs vary in their ease of use, how much they can be personalized for the individual user, the research evidence backing up their effectiveness, and the availability of interactive features. Several of the apps can be helpful for people to use on their own as well as in conjunction with traditional therapy.

Computerized versions of cognitive behavioral therapy (CBT) for anxiety (e.g., FearFighter, OCFighter/BTSteps, Panic Online, and Interapy) have been studied systematically and appear to be effective for a range of conditions, including panic disorder, phobias, and possibly obsessive-compulsive disorder.

DON'T GO IT ALONE

Spending time with others often reduces anxiety, possibly because it takes our focus off of ourselves and allows us to feel connected. Combining do-it-yourself strategies like meditation, exercise, and healthy eating with a social component can be a win-win. Enjoying an exhilarating walk with an empathic companion not only provides stress-reducing exercise; it allows you to discuss and sort out your worries, which can further reduce any feelings of anxiety. Sharing healthy meals with people, taking a group meditation class, or just calling a friend have all been shown to reduce anxiety, alleviate loneliness, and fight off depression.

Many people find support groups to be very helpful in calming their anxiety symptoms. Sharing your emotional experiences and learning about how others feel and cope can provide valuable insights for managing and lowering anxiety. The Anxiety and Depressive Association of America offers resources for finding local and online support groups for people experiencing various kinds of anxiety.

Taking medications or receiving medical treatment for anxiety does not preclude using self-help approaches. In fact, many people find that combining do-it-yourself strategies with conventional treatments for anxiety can be the most effective way to

AVAILABLE APPS FOR EASING ANXIETY

☐ *Breathe2Relax*: teaches breathing techniques to help with stress management

☐ *Headspace*: provides meditation techniques to reduce anxiety

☐ *Live OCD Free*: offers cognitive behavioral therapy (CBT) methods, including ERP (exposure response prevention) and a cognitive toolkit

☐ *MoodKit*: teaches general CBT concepts and helps with self-monitoring

☐ *Pacifica*: offers deep breathing and positive thinking techniques

☐ *Panic Relief*: helps people manage panic attacks using progressive muscle relaxation, deep breathing, and other exercises

☐ *Self-Help Anxiety Management*: monitors anxious thinking and behavior and provides self-help exercises

☐ *T2 Mood Tracker*: tracks emotional states over time

☐ *What's My M3*: rates anxiety symptoms and determines need for professional help

☐ *WorryWatch*: provides tools for monitoring worry and displaying cognitive distortions for people with generalized anxiety disorder relieve symptoms, recover more rapidly, and remain in remission.

Whether or not you are practicing self-help strategies, if anxiety is disrupting your everyday life, it can be essential to seek professional help. Even if you're not sure if you need it, it's best to err on the conservative side: when in doubt, always seek help. Many effective treatments are available for anxiety disorders, and untreated anxiety can result in serious consequences.

CHAPTER 3

Conventional Treatments That Work

> **Patient:** *"Doctor, my ears are ringing."*
> **Doctor:** *"Don't answer it."*
> —Milton Berle

IF ANXIETY SYMPTOMS ARE disrupting your life, then by definition you have an anxiety disorder. Fortunately, many conventional treatments can make a difference and improve your everyday functioning so you can feel calmer and experience more joy in your life.

* * *

David, a sixty-one-year-old attorney, came to see me because he was having trouble sleeping at night and concentrating at work. It was affecting his memory too—he'd begun forgetting clients' names and missing appointments. He'd tried relaxation techniques, exercising more, and meditation, but nothing seemed to help. He wanted me to prescribe him some Valium to relax.

As we talked, David seemed extremely anxious and glanced at his cell phone every minute or so. When I asked if anything had occurred lately that might be causing his unease, he told me that his wife died two years earlier, but he was doing fine now. In fact, he'd recently started dating again and had met several interesting women through an online dating site. With that, he grabbed his phone to check if he had any new texts.

David appeared to be obsessed with this dating site and was communicating with several women at once. His compulsive checking for texts and other messages was surely contributing to his anxiety symptoms, but I suspected there was something more going on.

He described his dates as being "all the same." The women would talk about themselves while David spent the whole time comparing them to his deceased wife to whom no one could measure up.

After several sessions, David came to realize that he was still mourning the loss of his wife, and he was using this dating-site mania as a distraction from his true feelings of loss. I prescribed him a low dose of an SSRI antidepressant, Zoloft, to help control his obsessive-compulsive behavior and reduce his anxiety, so he could focus at work. He responded well, and in therapy he was able to address his real feelings.

Soon David's anxiety symptoms abated, his memory improved, and he was able to sleep through the night.

*   *   *

Over the years, I've seen many patients like David who respond extremely well to the conventional anxiety treatments of medication, psychotherapy, or both. The specific form of treatment will depend on the particular type of anxiety disorder. Other factors that determine the treatment include the severity of symptoms, the level of support from family and friends, and the patient's motivation to get help.

Often the treating professional will use a combination of approaches, and the clinician's training and area of specialty will in part determine the form of treatment. Psychiatrists have a medical degree, which allows them to prescribe medications, while psychologists, marriage and family counselors, and other psychotherapists offer talk therapies but cannot prescribe medications.

WORKING WITH YOUR THERAPIST

Whether you require medication, psychotherapy, or both, establishing a collaborative relationship with your clinician will increase the likelihood that your treatment will be successful. When seeking help for anxiety, it's important to feel comfortable communicating with your doctor without feeling judged or dismissed. People often turn to their primary care physician first about their anxiety concerns. Although family physicians and internists can prescribe medicines for anxiety, a psychiatrist or psychologist with special training in treating anxiety disorders can be even more helpful in assessing, diagnosing, and treating your problem. Seeking out such a specialist is especially important if you find that you are not getting better while being treated by your primary care doctor.

Recommendations from a trusted friend or physician can help you find the right therapist for you. Prior to your first visit, write down specific questions that you wish to ask. Keeping a journal that details your symptoms and what triggers them will also help the doctor understand your anxiety better.

Before beginning a medication for anxiety, be sure your doctor knows about any other medications or over-the-counter drugs or supplements you are taking. Some medicines can cause side effects and so can some combinations of medications. If you do experience side effects, avoid stopping your medication without first consulting your physician. The drug may need to be tapered down rather than discontinued suddenly. Remember that medicines will have their greatest effect if you take them as prescribed by your doctor.

MEDICATIONS FOR TREATMENT OF ANXIETY

Several different types of medicines have been shown to be effective for a variety of anxiety disorders, and though they are not all classified as antianxiety drugs, they still relieve many anxiety symptoms. Of course, all medications have pros and cons. For example, benzodiazepines (e.g., Valium, Xanax) are effective for acute anxiety but some patients become physically and psychologically dependent on them. Antidepressants (e.g., Zoloft, Prozac) and buspirone (BuSpar) can control chronic symptoms, but they have to build up in one's system and have little if any effect during the first few weeks of treatment.

Whenever I prescribe medications to my patients, I try to use the smallest dosage in order to minimize potential side effects. I believe in starting low and going slow when I build the dosage level. This strategy is especially important when treating older adults who tend to be sensitive to even small doses of medicines. Also, if you do develop mild side effects such as an upset stomach or dry mouth, it's possible that your body will adjust to these discomforts after a few days or weeks.

Antidepressants

Although these medicines are called antidepressants, they are used to treat a variety of mental symptoms including anxiety. Antidepressants exert their effects by increasing the levels of serotonin, norepinephrine, and other neurotransmitters or brain messengers that regulate mood.

When starting an antidepressant, remember that it may take several weeks for mood effects to kick in. Patients unaware of this typical delay in treatment response may get discouraged and prematurely stop taking their medicine before they experience the benefits.

Frequently used antidepressants include the selective serotonin reuptake inhibitors (SSRIs), the serotonin-norepinephrine reuptake inhibitors (SNRIs), and the noradrenergic/specific serotonergic antidepressants (NaSSAs). Other antidepressants that are used less often include tricyclics, monoamine oxidase inhibitors (MAOIs), and trazodone. If an antidepressant medication is effective, the patient may remain on the medicine for months or even years.

Many of these medicines are effective in treating different forms of anxiety, while others are reserved for specific disorders. Both SSRIs and SNRIs work well for generalized anxiety, panic, social anxiety, and obsessive-compulsive disorders.

Side effects may develop when the medicine is initiated and vary among these medicines, but some "side effects" can actually improve symptoms. For example, a patient with anxiety and insomnia may respond well to a more sedating antidepressant like trazodone or Remeron taken at bedtime.

ANTIDEPRESSANTS USED TO TREAT ANXIETY

Category	Examples	Possible Side Effects
SSRI	Celexa (citalopram), Lexapro (escitalopram), Paxil (paroxetine), Prozac (fluoxetine), Zoloft (sertraline)	Nausea, upset stomach, weight gain, decreased libido, drowsiness
SNRI	Cymbalta (duloxetine hydrochloride), Effexor (venlafaxine), Pristiq (desvenlafaxine)	Nausea, insomnia, dizziness, drowsiness, weight loss, headaches
NaSSA	Remeron (mirtazapine)	Weight gain, drowsiness
Tricyclic	Anafranil (clomipramine), Elavil (amitriptyline), Norpramin (desipramine), Pamelor (nortriptyline)	Dry mouth, constipation, sweating, urinary retention, slowed heartbeat
MAOI	Nardil (phenelzine), Parnate (tranylcypromine)	Dizziness (when standing up), dry mouth, constipation, dangerous interaction with certain foods/drugs

Benzodiazepines

These medicines are very effective in managing acute anxiety since they calm the nervous system almost immediately. The early versions of benzodiazepines—drugs like Valium (diazepam), Klonopin (clonazepam), and Librium (chlordiazepoxide)—are long-acting medicines, which means that they stay in the body for extended periods of time. This can present a problem, particularly in older people, because levels of these drugs build up over time and can cause side effects. In more recent years, safer and shorter-acting drugs, such as Xanax (alprazolam) and Ativan (lorazepam), have become available and are less likely to accumulate in the body and cause long-term side effects.

Benzodiazepines are quite effective in treating panic attacks and other acute anxiety symptoms, but people may become dependent on them and develop side effects like drowsiness and confusion. I saw a patient several years ago who thought he had Alzheimer's disease. It turned out that he was taking 10 mg of Valium every day for more than a year. When I took him off the Valium, his symptoms of dementia resolved.

Benzodiazepines should not be mixed with alcohol and other sedating medicines. They can also interfere with a person's ability to drive: use of these medicines has been associated with higher rates of auto accidents.

Buspirone

Buspirone (BuSpar) is effective in treating symptoms of generalized anxiety disorder, and some studies show that it can be as effective as a benzodiazepine without the accompanying risk of dependence and drowsiness. This medicine does not have an immediate effect and can take several weeks before patients notice benefits. Unlike benzodiazepines, which are taken on an as-needed basis, BuSpar needs to be taken every day for it to reduce levels of anxiety. Possible side effects include dizziness, nausea, headaches, nervousness, lightheadedness, and constipation.

Anticonvulsants

Several of these medicines used to treat epilepsy and seizure disorders have also been shown to reduce symptoms of anxiety disorders. Neurontin (gabapentin) is useful in treating social anxiety and panic, while Lyrica (pregabalin) has been effective in treating generalized anxiety disorder. Side effects of Neurontin include unsteady gait, clumsiness, depressed mood, and restlessness; Lyrica may cause shortness of breath, chills, cough, and diarrhea.

Atypical Antipsychotics

This second generation of antipsychotic medication was developed to treat people who are out of touch with reality because of hallucinations or delusions.

Atypical antipsychotics have an effect on several neurotransmitters including serotonin which reduces many symptoms of anxiety. Examples include Seroquel (quetiapine), Zyprexa (olanzapine), and Risperdal (risperidone). Antipsychotic medicines may cause dry mouth, blurred vision, dizziness, weakness, restlessness, movement abnormalities, stiffness, and weight gain. Long-term use can lead to involuntary movements of the upper body and face.

Beta-Blockers

Beta-blockers such as Inderal (propranolol) and Tenormin (atenolol) are medicines originally developed to treat high blood pressure and heart arrhythmias. By blocking adrenaline, they inhibit the fight-or-flight response people experience under acute stress and control such physical symptoms of anxiety as rapid heart rate, sweating, and shakiness. They are particularly effective in treating symptoms associated with fear of public speaking and social phobia. By controlling the physical symptoms, patients also experience fewer psychological symptoms. Possible side effects include fatigue, cold hands, headache, and upset stomach.

CLASSES OF MEDICATION FOR TREATMENT OF ANXIETY

- antidepressants
- benzodiazepines
- buspirone
- anticonvulsants
- atypical antipsychotics
- beta-blockers

TALK THERAPIES

Several talk therapies or psychotherapies are available to treat anxiety, and your choice of a therapist will depend on the form of psychotherapy you are seeking. A variety of licensed mental health practitioners can provide talk therapies, including marriage and family counselors, psychologists, nurse practitioners, and psychiatrists. Some therapists are trained in cognitive behavioral therapy while others use a more psychodynamic or insight-oriented approach.

For anxiety disorders, several of these forms of therapy are considered to be "evidence-based," which means that systematic studies have been performed that demonstrate their effectiveness. The type of psychotherapy that makes sense will depend on the specific anxiety disorder being treated. Many psychotherapists focus on a particular form of talk therapy as well as a particular form of anxiety disorder, but most therapists are able to incorporate a combination of approaches into their practices. Regardless of the form of therapy, it is crucial that the therapist has a certain level of empathy so that the patient's emotional point of view is considered with sensitivity.

When choosing a therapist, you'll want to review the clinician's credentials and experience. It's also important to discuss your particular goals of the psychotherapy. Whenever you meet with a psychotherapist, the information discussed is always considered confidential except when there is a medical emergency or imminent danger to the patient or others.

Psychotherapy may be an alternative to treatment with medications, but the approaches are often used together. Medications can help alter the balance of brain messengers that lead to anxiety symptoms, while psychotherapy can provide a psychological perspective as well as specific cognitive tools to help avoid anxiety triggers and diminish symptoms once they occur.

Cognitive Behavioral Therapy (CBT)

CBT helps patients identify the triggers, thoughts, feelings, and behaviors that are linked to their anxiety by combining cognitive therapy and behavioral

FINDING A THERAPIST

The National Institute of Mental Health (NIMH) provides resources to help people find an appropriate therapist in their area. Below are examples of both professional and national advocacy organizations that list directories of professionals. You can easily find them online.

- **Academy of Cognitive Therapy**
- **Association for Behavioral Therapies**
- **American Academy of Child and Adolescent Psychiatry**
- **American Association for Geriatric Psychiatry**
- **American Psychiatric Association**
- **American Psychological Association**
- **Anxiety and Depression Association of America**
- **National Association of Social Workers**
- **Society of Clinical Psychology**
- **International OCD Foundation**
- **Mental Health America**
- **National Alliance on Mental Illness**

therapy. Systematic studies indicate that CBT is effective in treating panic disorder, phobias, social anxiety disorder, and generalized anxiety disorder.

The cognitive therapy component of CBT helps patients recognize and alter the distorted thoughts and beliefs that influence their behavior and increase their anxiety. Once the patient has identified his distorted thinking and its resulting behaviors, the therapist can help him examine and better understand the negative impact they have. This allows the patient to then develop and learn alternative, more-realistic thoughts and beliefs, which in turn lead to healthier behaviors.

Let's say a patient is unreasonably worried about her mother's health and constantly feels nervous about it. Her therapist might ask her to make a list of the real facts about her mother's health status and then compare that to a list of her exaggerated worries and thoughts. The process will help the patient accept and change the distorted thinking that influences her anxiety reactions.

Systematically writing down your reactions to your anxiety triggers will provide perspective and help you recognize how your automatic responses may be counterproductive and serve to reinforce your anxiety symptoms. This kind of recognition is the first step to learning healthier responses and breaking the chronic anxiety cycle.

The behavior component of CBT involves changing the patient's behaviors in order to alter their thoughts, beliefs, and feelings. Let's say a person has a habit of eating cookies in bed every night, and this causes him to feel guilty, remorseful, and anxious about his weight the next day. The therapist would

TRY THIS

To get a better idea of how CBT works, think of a situation that makes you anxious. It could be a social setting or any number of things. Perhaps you have a fear of spiders. Consider what triggers your fear (e.g., finding a spider on your bed, seeing a movie about spiders); describe your thoughts (spiders may be crawling on me right now) and feelings (fear, panic, desperation) associated with it as well as how you generally respond (hyperventilation, panic attack). See the example below and then fill in the row below the example with your own triggers, thoughts, feelings, and behaviors.

Trigger	Thoughts	Feelings	Behaviors
Finding out you weren't invited to a party.	What did I do to make that person hate me?	I feel insecure that nobody likes me.	Avoid social activities; keep checking Facebook.
_____	_____	_____	_____
_____	_____	_____	_____
_____	_____	_____	_____

encourage the patient to alter his cookie-eating behavior—perhaps by writing down exactly what he is feeling when the urge to eat cookies hits or maybe by simply throwing out all the cookies in the house. If the patient can agree to try this change, even just once, the reduced anxiety he experiences the next morning will reinforce his new healthy behavior and motivate him to skip the cookies again the following night.

Exposure Therapy

When we fear something, it is our natural instinct to avoid it, but that very avoidance often serves to reinforce our fears. Exposure therapy is a form of behavioral therapy that helps patients face their anxieties through exercises that expose them—usually gradually—to situations or objects that stir up their anxiety.

With gradual exposure training, patients confront their fears in baby steps using systematic desensitization, which involves creating a hierarchy of feared scenarios. The patient is exposed to the least frightening scenario first. Once she overcomes her fear in that setting, she then moves on to the next most frightening experience. This gradual increase in exposure to a feared situation will serve to desensitize her to her fears.

Perhaps a patient suffers from agoraphobia and refuses to leave his house. His therapist may first help him open the front door and stand in the doorway.

Once he's comfortable there, he would move on to step on the porch, then walk slowly to the sidewalk, and so on. The exercises may first involve imagining the feared scenarios before moving on to actual *in vivo* or real-life exposure.

PSYCHOTHERAPIES FOR TREATING ANXIETY

- cognitive behavioral therapy (CBT)
- exposure therapy
- relaxation therapy
- acceptance and commitment therapy (ACT)
- eye movement desensitization and reprocessing (EMDR)
- hypnosis
- psychodynamic psychotherapy

For a patient who fears swimming in a pool, a gradual exposure approach might first involve dipping a toe and then a whole foot into a swimming pool. Eventually, as that person becomes more comfortable with his body in the water, he can get closer and closer to overcoming his fear of swimming.

An alternate exposure approach is called flooding, wherein the patient is exposed to the most feared situation all at once. For instance, the patient who fears swimming would simply jump into the pool. The therapeutic coach in this situation would encourage the patient to jump in or possibly even push the patient into the pool. By doing this, the patient is forced to suddenly overcome her fear of swimming. This more drastic approach can sometimes be effective, but it also poses the risk of worsening the individual's anxieties, escalating her fears, and harming the bond between patient and therapist.

Relaxation Therapy

Effective relaxation techniques can be learned on your own with self-help approaches or by working with a professional therapist. Whether it's autogenic training, progressive relaxation, or meditation, it can be easier to learn these methods from a professional "guide" before trying them on one's own.

The particular emphasis of relaxation therapy will vary depending on the experience and orientation of the therapist. However, if you have an interest in a specific technique, you may wish to ask your therapist whether they have experience using that approach. For these strategies to be effective, it's essential to develop enough of a comfort level so that you can eventually practice them on your own without the direct guidance of the therapist.

Relaxation techniques complement other therapy methods. For example, a patient undergoing gradual exposure or desensitization therapy can use mindfulness techniques or deep breathing to help control both psychological and physical symptoms of anxiety triggered by the exposure therapy.

Acceptance and Commitment Therapy (ACT)

Some therapists use a strategy represented by the acronym **ACT**:

- Accept your reactions and stay in the moment.
- Choose a new direction that is consistent with your goals and values.
- Take action—follow through with new behaviors more in line with reaching your goals.

This form of therapy combines cognitive training with mindfulness techniques. The ultimate goal of ACT is to help people manage their anxiety by developing more psychological flexibility. ACT does not aim to completely eliminate a patient's psychological discomfort but instead teaches them to accept and live with anxiety-provoking situations while making a commitment to not overreact to their anxious feelings. Several systematic studies indicate that ACT is effective in treating anxiety disorders, and many experts believe it is comparable to CBT in its effectiveness.

Many practitioners of ACT believe that patients with anxiety disorders face four main psychological challenges and often use the acronym **FEAR** to represent them:

Fusion with thoughts
Evaluation of the anxiety-provoking experience
Avoidance of the experience
Reason-giving for inappropriate behavior

Eye Movement Desensitization and Reprocessing (EMDR)

Often used to treat various forms of anxiety as well as posttraumatic stress disorder, EMDR involves asking patients to remember a traumatic experience and any negative thoughts and feelings it invoked while at the same time performing specific eye movements. EMDR practitioners may use various approaches to stimulate the patient's eye movements to achieve the desired therapeutic effect.

Some therapists use ruler-shaped boards to get the patient to track a light that travels back and forth along the ruler; others simply move their finger back and forth in front of the patient's eyes while the patient recalls the traumatic event. Exactly how EMDR works is unclear, but a recent functional MRI study indicated that when research subjects make these eye movements while recalling a traumatic experience, neural activity increases between brain regions that process emotions. Although EMDR is used to relieve anxiety symptoms, it does not appear to be as effective as exposure therapy for treating specific phobias and panic disorders.

Hypnosis

The therapeutic effects of hypnosis or hypnotherapy can have a great impact on reducing anxiety. Patients are induced into a heightened state of awareness wherein they can block out distractions and become receptive to suggestions that can help them change, whether they want to quit smoking or conquer a fear of flying. In addition to its use in treating pain, obesity, and other medical conditions, hypnosis has been used to treat a range of anxiety disorders such as generalized anxiety, agoraphobia, and panic. Systematic research indicates hypnosis is especially effective when combined with CBT.

After an initial induction phase, hypnotherapists use imagery and relaxation prompts to intensify the patient's hypnotic state. When a deeply focused and calm state is achieved, the therapist then makes suggestions to help the patient alter his or her anxious thoughts and behaviors and remain relaxed after the hypnosis session. Once they get the hang of it, many people use self-hypnosis techniques to induce these states without the help of a therapist.

Psychodynamic Psychotherapy

Psychodynamic or insight-oriented psychotherapy evolved from classic psychoanalysis and can be very helpful in reducing anxiety. The therapist helps patients become aware of the thoughts and feelings that shape their behavior, as well as gain perspective and understanding of how their past experiences influence their present feelings and actions. This form of therapy helps patients examine unresolved conflicts in order to improve their symptoms. Many clinicians trained in psychodynamic theory and treatment may combine this approach with CBT and other interventions, including medications and talk therapy.

CHAPTER 4

Alternative Therapies

*Be careful about reading health
books. You may die of a misprint.*
　　　　　　　　　　—Mark Twain

WHEN ANXIETY SUFFERERS SEEK relief, they often try
do-it-yourself strategies before turning to their
doctor for more conventional treatments. Then if
nothing seems to work, their next step may be to
try alternative therapies like acupuncture or reflexology. But what one person considers an alternative
treatment can seem like a first-line intervention to
another. There are many anxious patients who try
alternative treatments first, and they are becoming
more and more mainstream.

Some do-it-yourself strategies such as meditation or yoga can also be categorized as alternative
treatments for anxiety, and conventional medical
practitioners may recommend these approaches in

conjunction with evidence-based medicines or psychotherapies. When alternative approaches are used
together with traditional medical interventions, they
are considered complementary treatments.

Today, alternative and complementary therapies
for anxiety are even more popular than conventional
treatments. One survey of more than two thousand
respondents indicated that 51 percent of those with
anxiety attacks had received conventional therapy
from a professional, whereas 89 percent had pursued
complementary or alternative therapies.

Although the beneficial results of several alternative therapies are encouraging, many have not yet
been studied systematically, so whether they actually work better than placebo treatments is not yet
known. However, that fact doesn't deter the many
patients who do get relief from alternative techniques. In fact, studies of placebo treatments have
shown that they can offer temporary benefits—some
researchers found a 30 percent response rate for placebo treatments. If a patient truly believes that their
alternative treatment is working, it can actually be
effective for a while. Unfortunately, over time, the
placebo effect wears off.

A possible danger of pursuing alternative therapies first, however, is that the anxiety sufferer may
delay getting a conventional treatment that could
effectively relieve their symptoms very quickly.

When patients or families ask me about alternative therapies, I inform them of what we do and do not know about their effectiveness and safety. I encourage people to try some alternative as well as do-it-yourself strategies, but when asked, I recommend conventional treatments.

DIETARY AND HERBAL SUPPLEMENTS

Also termed nutraceuticals or herbal remedies, many people use supplements to treat their anxiety symptoms. If you do, it's important to discuss this with your doctor, particularly if you also take other medications. Remember that these remedies can interact with certain medications to cause serious side effects.

Dietary supplements have been regulated in the United States since 1994 by the Dietary Supplement Health and Education Act, which set forth standards for manufacturers who are responsible for the truthfulness of label claims. Although several supplements have been tested and shown to be more effective than placebo, the consumer still faces challenges when deciding whether to take a particular supplement.

Quality control of supplements is also an issue. Most available supplements have not been systematically tested against a placebo treatment. Just because a dietary supplement is natural, it doesn't necessarily mean it is safe, and health risks can emerge from drug interactions or contaminants. Problems including excess bleeding, pain, insomnia, and even serious drug interactions have been reported with various supplements. For example, ingesting ginkgo biloba along with ibuprophen can slow blood clotting and lead to bruising and bleedings. Also, ginkgo can affect insulin secretion, making it potentially dangerous for diabetics.

DID YOU KNOW?

- According to the CDC, over one half of Americans use dietary supplements.

- Several supplements have undergone double-blind placebo-controlled studies showing that their benefits are greater than placebo.

- Most supplements do not contain all of what's listed on the label.

- Several supplements on the shelf don't work at all.

Many of the available supplements and herbal remedies used to treat anxiety are described below, but when deciding which one may be right for you, a knowledgeable pharmacist or physician can be very helpful. You might also check reliable online resources, such as the National Center for Complementary and Alternative Medicine (nccam.nih.gov) and the Natural Medicines Comprehensive Database (www.naturaldatabase.com).

Inositol

A form of sugar or glucose that is naturally present in our diets, inositol is a supplement that influences several anxiety-related brain messengers, including serotonin. Some studies have shown that it is as effective as some SSRI antidepressants in treating panic attacks, and it may help patients with obsessive-compulsive disorder. Side effects are generally minimal but similar to those of SSRIs, including loss of appetite, nausea, diarrhea, and dizziness. It should not be combined with an SSRI, and recommended doses range from twelve to eighteen grams per day.

Kava

An herb from the South Pacific that has been used as a social drink and in ceremonial rituals for hundreds of years, kava extracts are thought to influence the GABA brain messenger system to relieve anxiety. Short-term use may improve symptoms of generalized anxiety. However, despite some promising results for the treatment of anxiety symptoms, safety concerns have led to bans of kava in many countries. Although it is available in the United States, the FDA has issued safety warnings about its risks, particularly for liver damage. Alcohol and medicines that affect the liver will increase the risk of liver damage when used with kava.

L-lysine/L-arginine Combination

Amino acids such as lysine and arginine are building blocks for brain messengers or neurotransmitters involved in anxiety symptoms. Several studies have demonstrated antianxiety benefits for a combination of L-lysine and L-arginine. Side effects are generally minimal.

Ginkgo Biloba

Extracts of these leaves have been used to treat age-related memory loss with varying success. Initial studies of potential benefits for patients with generalized anxiety disorder are encouraging but require follow-up. Potential side effects include an upset stomach and possibly increased bleeding.

Magnesium

This positively charged ion is involved in many body functions that are linked to anxiety symptoms. Several studies have demonstrated magnesium's possible antianxiety effects for generalized anxiety disorder and other forms of anxiety. It is often combined with various vitamins, so it is unclear whether magnesium alone provides the benefits or if it must be combined with other substances. Magnesium has few, if any, side effects.

Marijuana

Initial studies suggest that cannabinoids, the non-psychoactive components of marijuana, may reduce anxiety symptoms in patients with PTSD or panic disorder. More research is recommended because of the potential for side effects and abuse.

Passionflower

Some small studies suggest that passionflower may reduce anxiety. One investigation in patients with generalized anxiety disorder showed that benefits of passionflower were equivalent to those of a benzo-diazepine antianxiety medicine. However, scientists have been unable to determine the precise passion-flower ingredient that provides the benefits, so the consistency of each product varies. Side effects are generally mild and may include dizziness, drowsi-ness, and confusion.

St. John's Wort

Extracts from this flowering plant have been used to treat depression, anxiety, and insomnia. Its benefits may stem from action on serotonin, dopamine, and the GABA brain messenger systems. Although inves-tigations in patients with depression are promising, systematic studies in patients with anxiety have not demonstrated benefits. St. John's wort may cause side effects when taken with several medicines, including anti-inflammatory drugs, antidepressants, statins, and proton pump inhibitors. The available evidence does not support a role for St John's wort in the treatment of anxiety disorders.

DIETARY AND HERBAL SUPPLEMENTS USED TO REDUCE ANXIETY

The amount of scientific evidence supporting the antianxiety benefits of these various supplements ranges from controlled studies demonstrating benefits beyond placebo to little or no evidence of any benefits at all.

EVIDENCE FOR BENEFITS

- inositol, kava, l-lysine/l-arginine combination

SOME ENCOURAGING RESULTS

- ginkgo biloba, magnesium, marijuana, passionflower

LIMITED OR NO SCIENTIFIC EVIDENCE OF BENEFITS

- Bach flower essences, bacopa, California poppy, chamomile, lavender, lemon balm, omega-3 fatty acids, St. John's wort, theanine, valerian

NEUROMODULATION

Neuromodulation is a growing area of mental health therapeutics that encompasses several technologies that stimulate or suppress brain nerves in order to reduce mental symptoms. Recently approved by the FDA for certain indications, including depression, some of these brain stimulation methods have minimal side effects compared with medication and tend to show positive results in treatment-resistant cases. These noninvasive approaches—including magnetic stimulation, ultrasound waves, and electrical impulses—are designed to jump-start key neural circuits controlling anxiety in the brain.

One of the more popular neuromodulation treatments, repetitive transcranial magnetic stimulation (rTMS), uses magnets to activate brain neural circuits. It has been shown to be effective in treating symptoms but is limited in that it cannot reach regions located deep within the brain.

Transcranial direct-current stimulation (tDCS) uses a simple device involving the placement of electrodes on the head to excite or reduce neuronal activity, and recent research points to its promise in treating anxiety. One study demonstrated that tDCS is particularly effective in relieving anxiety symptoms in patients with obsessive-compulsive disorder.

Cranial electrotherapy stimulation (CES) uses a palm-sized device to send small electric currents across the brain and has been used for treating both anxiety and insomnia. One advantage of this approach is that patients can use the device at home, but some recent studies have begun to question the effectiveness of the method.

One promising method known as low-intensity focused ultrasound pulsation (LIFUP) uses ultrasound energy pulses to excite or suppress brain cell activity. The technique provides noninvasive, focused ultrasound energy through the skull and can be used with functional MRI to target specific brain regions implicated in anxiety symptoms.

NEUROMODULATION TECHNOLOGIES THAT MAY REDUCE ANXIETY

- repetitive transcranial magnetic stimulation (rTMS)
- cranial electrotherapy stimulation (CES)
- transcranial direct-current stimulation (tDCS)
- low-intensity focused ultrasound pulsation (LIFUP)

BIOFEEDBACK AND NEUROFEEDBACK

Biofeedback and neurofeedback train patients to adjust their reactions to anxiety by monitoring their own physiological stress responses. During stress and anxiety states, heart rate increases, hands become cold and clammy, muscles tense, and brain waves measured by electroencephalograms (EEGs) show increases in beta waves. Also, the stressed-out brain shows a shift in activity from the amygdala emotional center under the temples to the frontal lobe's thinking brain region.

With biofeedback, patients receive visual or auditory input from noninvasive sensors indicating physiological changes during stress and learn how to control their brain's activity to achieve and maintain a calm and focused state. Neurofeedback is a form of biofeedback that specifically uses EEG sensors to monitor brain wave activity. A sound or visual cue will provide either positive or negative feedback. Although it has been used for a variety of anxiety symptoms and some people have reported benefits, scientific evidence supporting its use is limited.

MASSAGE AND BODYWORK

Massage and other forms of bodywork help a lot of people relax and reduce their symptoms of anxiety. Anyone who has received a good massage knows how nice and relaxing it can feel, but just how it works to relieve mental anxiety is not entirely clear. It is possible that massage alters brain neurotransmitters involved in anxiety symptoms as well as the level of stress hormones in the body. Also, if the treatment relieves pain, any anxiety associated with that pain will likely decline.

Research has shown that moderate pressure massage provides temporary pain relief for people suffering from fibromyalgia or rheumatoid arthritis. In addition to reducing anxiety levels, moderate pressure massage alters brain wave patterns measured by EEGs and reduces levels of the stress hormone cortisol. Studies using functional MRI indicate that moderate pressure massage alters brain activity in the amygdala, hypothalamus, and frontal lobe. These are all brain regions that control and regulate stress and emotion.

Many people endorse the benefits of various types of bodywork therapy including Reiki, Bowen technique, reflexology, aromatherapy, and chiropractic treatment. As yet, systematic studies confirming the specific benefits of these different approaches over placebo treatments have not been confirmed. However, even without such evidence, these approaches have reportedly helped many individuals.

Acupuncture, another form of bodywork imported from the Far East and practiced for thousands of years, has been used to treat medical conditions like nausea and pain. Some scientific research does point to the benefits of acupuncture and acupressure in treating various anxiety symptoms as well as insomnia.

OTHER APPROACHES

Many other alternative therapies have been recommended to help people remain calm and manage their symptoms of anxiety, ranging from homeopathic treatments to prayer. Scientific evidence supporting these approaches is limited, but they still seem to help some individuals.

I often recommend that anxiety sufferers try one or more of these approaches, especially since they have minimal risk. Systematic studies have shown that laughter or humor therapy can enhance mood and quality of life. Listening to music, pursuing hobbies, and volunteering are just some examples of potentially fun and relaxing activities that can distract us from our feelings of anxiety and help us remain calmer under stress.

ALTERNATIVE STRATEGIES FOR REDUCING ANXIETY SYMPTOMS

- *dietary and herbal supplements*
  - ◦ inositol, kava, l-lysine/l-arginine combination
- *neuromodulation*
  - ◦ rTMS, tDCS, CES, LIFUP
- *biofeedback and neurofeedback*
- *bodywork*
  - ◦ massage, acupuncture, acupressure
- *other approaches*
  - ◦ laughter, hobbies, listening to music, prayer, spiritual pursuits, pets, volunteering

Many alternative treatments may help reduce stress and anxiety, and they also work well in conjunction with conventional therapies to relieve symptoms. Keep in mind that if you do pursue an alternative treatment, do not allow it to delay a trial of a conventional therapy that has been shown to alleviate anxiety. Also, if a particular therapy sounds too good to be true, that may very well be the case. Before beginning an alternative approach, you may want to investigate whether any scientific studies have been performed to show that the approach works better than placebo.

CHAPTER 5

Worried Sick

Generalized Anxiety Disorder

> *The reason that worry kills more*
> *people than work is that more people*
> *worry than work.*
>
> —Robert Frost

BRUCE TRIED TO GET comfortable in a chair with his hands resting in his lap. The voice from the guided meditation app instructed him to close his eyes and breathe slowly and deeply through his nose.

"Feel the cool air enter your nostrils as you inhale," the meditation guide said. "Notice the warm air flowing out as you exhale, and stay focused on your breath."

Bruce tried to follow the instructions, but his mind kept wandering—was his son going to get into a decent graduate school? Would the boss bust his chops at work again today? Could that pain in his forehead be another sinus infection coming on?

He tried focusing on his breathing, but that only made matters worse. Was he breathing deep enough? Was too much oxygen going to his brain? Bruce recalled smoking cigarettes in college and wondered if he was going to get cancer as a punishment. He knew that wasn't likely, but those kinds of thoughts kept creeping into his mind.

Bruce struggled to bring his mind back to his breath coming in and out, but a moment later, his thoughts were off to the races again. This stupid meditation was making him *more* anxious. Finally, he opened his eyes—his heart was racing, and he was out of breath. He had to splash some water on his face to calm himself down.

*   *   *

Bruce, fifty, had been a high-strung person all his life. For as long as he could remember, he'd been cautious about doing anything that seemed risky, whether it was playing football, horseback riding, or biking to the beach with the other kids. He described his mind as a "worry magnet"—if there were anything out there to fret about, his mind would latch on to it for dear life. Bruce knew that his constant rumination and lack of confidence in his own decisions contributed to his insomnia and persistent fatigue.

Despite his constant "free-floating anxiety" as Bruce liked to call it, he was able to move on with his life—he was married with two children, worked as an accountant, and enjoyed his small circle of friends. But he was always looking for ways to remain calm and reduce his worries.

Bruce never liked going to the doctor because he didn't want to hear any bad news, but eventually he saw his internist about his anxiety problem. The doctor prescribed an antidepressant medication, but Bruce only took it for a few weeks because he couldn't bear the headaches, nausea, sexual dysfunction, and other side effects. Besides, he didn't really feel depressed, he just felt incredibly anxious.

If Bruce's internist had been a bit more psychologically savvy, he might have been able to give Bruce a name for his cluster of symptoms—generalized anxiety disorder (GAD). Unlike other anxiety problems such as phobias or obsessive-compulsive disorder, GAD has no one obvious cause or set of symptoms; therefore, many times, it goes undiagnosed and untreated for years or even lifetimes.

Approximately 10 percent of all people will develop generalized anxiety disorder at some point in life. If you are a woman, you are twice as likely to have the condition, and everyone's risk peaks in middle age. People of European descent or from developed countries have a greater risk than those from other continents or nondeveloped countries.

As with most anxiety disorders, the exact cause is not understood, but genetics plays a role since the condition can run in families. Also, an individual's temperament contributes to risk: if you tend to be negative, timid, or avoidant of anything perceived as dangerous, you are predisposed to develop a generalized anxiety disorder.

Brain chemistry research on GAD indicates that certain neural circuits involved in thinking and emotional responses become overactive while others become less active. Trauma, environmental stress, and psychological loss may contribute to symptoms. Medical illnesses, caffeine, nicotine, and some medications can also worsen symptoms.

Many of Bruce's symptoms may be familiar to you. Perhaps you've experimented with some self-help strategies that didn't seem to do much. Your friends may tease you about being a worrier. You may play down your symptoms and joke about how you just like to be cautious. Or perhaps you don't even think of your tendency to worry as a problem—your negative attitudes about future concerns may have been around for so long that you just think of them as normal.

Lots of people like Bruce suffer from GAD their whole lives without receiving proper treatment. Although they may struggle for years to find ways to alleviate their discomfort, it's hard to know what to do about their symptoms until they figure out what condition they actually have. That was one of the first things I learned in medical school—you can't design a treatment until you have a diagnosis.

SYMPTOMS OF
GENERALIZED ANXIETY DISORDER

Experiencing some degree of anxiety is a normal aspect of life. If those transient feelings become excessive, chronic, or interfere with a person's ability to function effectively, a generalized anxiety disorder may be present. Patients with GAD tend to fret about almost anything that might happen in the future. They may even worry about being worried. They can become preoccupied with their physical health or just feel tired all the time for no reason.

A GAD patient's perceived trigger of the anxiety can also vary from time to time and is often susceptible to daily events, such as world news, personal losses, or any kind of change—both positive and negative. Children and adolescents may focus on school performance, nuclear war, need for approval, or perfectionism, while older adults may become apprehensive about memory slips and physical decline.

DO YOU HAVE GAD?

Ask yourself if you have any of the following symptoms. If you find yourself checking off several of the boxes, GAD may be the source of your unease.

☐ easily startled

☐ chronic fatigue

☐ trouble concentrating

☐ headaches

☐ trembling

☐ persistent rumination

☐ indecisiveness

☐ insomnia

☐ muscle tension

☐ irritability

Bruce knew me from when I treated his father for Alzheimer's disease, and when he absolutely couldn't stand his symptoms anymore, he sought me out and made an appointment. As I listened to him describe his anxiety symptoms, a diagnosis of generalized anxiety disorder seemed like a no-brainer, but there were other possible contributing factors to rule out first. Bruce's attempt at meditation failed because he was too easily distracted whenever he tried it, which

**DIAGNOSTIC FEATURES OF
GENERALIZED ANXIETY DISORDER**

- excessive anxiety and worry

- difficulty controlling worry

- three or more of the following:
    - feeling restless, edgy, or keyed up
    - often tired
    - trouble concentrating or mind going blank
    - irritability
    - muscle tension
    - sleep problems

 The symptoms

- cause significant stress or interfere with social or occupational functioning and

- can't be explained by another physical or mental
  problem.

could have indicated an attention deficit disorder.
His shortness of breath and episodic nature of his
symptoms suggested possible panic attacks.

However, after getting a more detailed history of
what he'd been experiencing, GAD was the most
likely diagnosis. Bruce's free-floating anxiety drifted
from one concern to the next, and that had become
his standard mental state. He had gotten used to

it, and it seemed like no matter what he did in life, in the back of his mind, there was always a concern that things could go wrong at any moment. We reviewed the diagnostic criteria for a GAD diagnosis, and Bruce met almost every one.

Symptoms of generalized anxiety disorder vary among individuals, and sometimes patients have features of several anxiety disorders simultaneously. Bruce had trouble controlling his anxiety throughout the day, and even when he enjoyed a momentary reprieve from worry, he would fret about when the next bad thing would occur. This anticipatory quality of worry differentiates it from fear, which is a distressing emotion triggered by impending danger rather concern about some future hypothetical event.

IS IT REALLY GAD OR SOMETHING ELSE?

Although Bruce's symptoms were typical of a generalized anxiety disorder, sometimes another psychiatric disorder or medical illness may be causing the symptom cluster or syndrome. Many patients who have major depression also experience anxiety symptoms. They too suffer from irritability, insomnia, anxiety, and fatigue, and this may be why Bruce's internist thought it was depression. Also, many GAD symptoms overlap with other anxiety disorders, such as social anxiety and panic disorder.

Bruce did not appear depressed to me, and he didn't have other features typical of major depression like appetite loss or feelings of guilt. Also, his insomnia was more representative of an anxiety disorder than depression—he had trouble falling asleep at bedtime, whereas depressed people complain of awakening in the middle of the night or too early in the morning and being unable to fall back to sleep.

When I questioned Bruce about panic attacks, it didn't seem like a big issue for him. Social anxiety didn't appear to be the problem either—Bruce felt comfortable with friends and family and even meeting new people occasionally, despite his natural distrust of strangers.

Physical symptoms, including intermittent shortness of breath, fatigue, dizziness, and upset stomach, are common in generalized anxiety disorder, and Bruce had several physical complaints. Sometimes physical illnesses can trigger anxiety symptoms and can be the underlying cause of many anxiety disorder symptoms. I conferred with Bruce's internist, and we made sure that his laboratory tests were up to date. In older or middle-aged individuals like Bruce, I am particularly concerned about physical or mental symptoms being a clue to an underlying medical condition because age increases a person's risk of medical illnesses such as cancer, diabetes, and heart disease. We ran some blood tests, checked his cardiogram, and determined that no physical illnesses could explain Bruce's symptoms.

PHYSICAL SYMPTOMS OF GENERALIZED ANXIETY

- muscular pain, tension

- headache

- tightness of muscles

- ringing in the ears

- chest pain

- fatigue

- sweating

- trembling and shaking

- shortness of breath

- dizziness

- numbness and tingling

- rapid heart rate

- upset stomach

In Bruce's case, his attempts at self-help strategies seemed to backfire. After trying both mindfulness and transcendental meditation on his own, he gave up on meditation because it just made him feel more anxious and left him feeling like a failure. When I suggested an anxiety medicine, Bruce was afraid to try it because of the bad reaction he had to the antidepressant. He wanted to try everything else before turning to meds.

TRYING ALTERNATIVE TREATMENTS

Many anxiety disorders, including GAD, can sometimes respond well to alternative therapies. Deep breathing exercises, biofeedback, yoga, tai chi, meditation, and hypnosis can be beneficial in reducing symptoms. Healthy lifestyle habits that promote brain health also help reduce symptoms of anxiety.

Several nutritional supplements have been used to treat generalized anxiety as well. Kava has shown some benefits, but it can cause serious liver damage, so it is no longer available in Canada and some European countries. In the United States, the Food and Drug Administration has issued warnings regarding its safety. Until more research is available, it is best to avoid kava, especially if you take other medicines that can affect your liver (including Tylenol) or have liver problems.

Although valerian has shown positive results in some studies, the findings are inconsistent, and it also can cause liver problems. Some small studies have shown evidence for the calming effects of passionflower. Possible side effects include drowsiness, dizziness, and confusion. Theanine is an amino acid that is present in green tea and several supplements. Some studies demonstrate its calming effects, but there is limited evidence for its effectiveness for generalized anxiety disorder.

SUPPLEMENTS / HERBAL REMEDIES USED TO TREAT GAD

POSSIBLY EFFECTIVE

- German chamomile, ginkgo, kava, lavender, lemon balm, melatonin, passionflower

INSUFFICIENT EVIDENCE FOR EFFECTIVENESS

- 5-HTP (5-Hydroxytryptophan), ashwagandha, bacopa, bergamot, bitter orange, California poppy, echinacea, guarana, hawthorn, holy basil, magnesium, motherwort, rhodiola, skullcap, St. John's wort, theanine, valerian, wine, yohimbe

---

Because generalized anxiety can affect people throughout life, it is important to find a treatment plan and a coping strategy that work and stick to them. You may feel better in one day or one week, but the symptoms will likely recur if you cut back on your relaxation exercises or healthy lifestyle strategies.

Joining an anxiety support group can help reduce feelings of isolation and provide a better understanding of your own experiences and those of others. Staying socially connected with empathic friends and relatives also helps people gain perspective on their symptoms and avoid isolation.

LIFESTYLE HABITS THAT MAY BENEFIT GENERALIZED ANXIETY DISORDER

- Stay physically active by creating a daily routine of walking, jogging, or any aerobic exercise.

- Limit alcohol and sedative medicines.

- Cut back on coffee consumption.

- Quit smoking.

- Make sleep a priority.

- Consume a healthy diet that includes fish, whole grains, fruits, and vegetables.

CONVENTIONAL THERAPIES FOR GENERALIZED ANXIETY DISORDER

The good news is that treatments for generalized anxiety can be very effective. Unfortunately, many

GAD sufferers, in part because of their anxious condition, are apprehensive about seeking professional help. When left untreated, the symptoms of generalized anxiety can escalate and lead to chronic insomnia, fatigue, substance abuse, and depression as well as contribute to physical illnesses such as heart disease and bowel disorders.

Bruce's trial of several alternative strategies failed to reduce his symptoms. Yoga bored him, he was afraid of acupuncture needles, and he couldn't relax enough for hypnosis. Because he'd already gotten over the hump of asking for help, I was able to encourage him to keep working with me.

Often the hardest step for anxious patients is making the first appointment with a mental-health professional, even though conventional treatments for generalized anxiety, including psychotherapy and medications, can be very effective. With psychological counseling, patients are able to discuss the sources of their anxiety and gain perspective on their symptoms. This allows them to develop more successful coping strategies.

Once Bruce and I broke the ice, he began to trust me and feel more at ease. Knowing his fear of medication, my initial approach was to use talk therapy in order to help Bruce revisit his attempts at meditation and help get his symptoms under control.

I described some of the real brain effects of meditation, including the work of Harvard scientists who taught volunteers to meditate using focused attention on physical sensations such as deep breathing. The scientists found that after eight weeks, the meditating volunteers had larger volumes of grey matter in their brain's hippocampal memory-control region. Understanding how the process can actually change neural circuits motivated Bruce to give it another try.

Bruce let me guide him through some meditation exercises and these helped calm him. I told Bruce that he should expect his mind to wander, and when it did, simply recognizing it and nonjudgmentally bringing his attention back to his breathing was enough to alter his neural circuits and reduce his anxiety. When Bruce stopped criticizing himself about his mind wandering, he became more comfortable and successful with his meditation.

We also began a course of cognitive behavioral therapy, which has been shown to be one of the most effective psychotherapies for generalized anxiety disorder. Patients need not worry that their psychotherapy will last for years and years: often short-term periods (weeks to months) of cognitive behavioral therapy are enough to help the patient learn to recognize and change thought patterns and behaviors that lead to anxiety. It helps patients to put their worries into perspective and reduce any distorted thinking.

THE ANXIETY TRIPLE THREAT: COMBINING PSYCHOTHERAPY, MEDICATION, AND ALTERNATIVE STRATEGIES

Several types of medicines are effective in reducing symptoms of generalized anxiety, including anti-anxiety drugs and some antidepressants. For some people, combining psychotherapy and medication treatment is the most effective strategy. Healthy life-style strategies also reduce symptoms of generalized anxiety.

Bruce was beginning to get some relief from his worries through meditation. He also used it to help him settle down and sleep better at night. The cognitive behavioral therapy also reduced his anxiety symptoms. By figuring out what triggered his worries and the thoughts and feelings associated with them, he was able to begin to alter his responses. Bruce was progressing, but not at a pace that satisfied him and he was still suffering from some of his symptoms.

I revisited the idea of trying a medication for a while. Although I didn't think it was necessary to prescribe a benzodiazepine or other tranquilizer, which often induced side effects, there were other types of first-line medicines that would likely improve Bruce's symptoms. I finally convinced him to try BuSpar, an antianxiety drug that affects neurotransmitters in the brain and has very few side effects if any. After a

few weeks, the effects of the medicine kicked in, and
Bruce felt better than he had in years.

MEDICATIONS FOR TREATMENT OF GENERALIZED ANXIETY DISORDER

- *Minor tranquilizers or benzodiazepines* can help reduce some of the physical symptoms of anxiety and are used in severe cases or for brief periods to relieve acute anxiety. Beware, however, that they can become habit-forming and can cause problems when used with alcohol or other sedating medications.
    - *Examples*: alprazolam (Xanax), chlordiazepoxide (Librium), diazepam (Valium), and lorazepam (Ativan)

- Buspirone (BuSpar) is an antianxiety medicine that may take several weeks to have an effect. The side effects are minimal, and it is nonaddictive.

- *Antidepressants*
    - Selective serotonin reuptake inhibitors (SSRIs) and serotonin-norepinephrine reuptake inhibitor (SNRIs) are first-line treatments and may take weeks to become effective.
    - *Examples*: sertraline (Zoloft), fluoxetine (Prozac), escitalopram (Lexapro), duloxetine (Cymbalta), venlafaxine (Effexor XR), and paroxetine (Paxil)

In addition to medication, therapy, and meditation, I encouraged Bruce to try getting more exercise. He had read that physical exercise can help people with depression, but it never occurred to him that it also may reduce symptoms of anxiety disorders. He lived in the foothills of Los Angeles, so it was easy for him to start taking brisk walks up and down the hills to get daily cardiovascular conditioning in the evenings. The regular exercise improved his sleep and daytime energy levels and seemed to further reduce his anxiety symptoms.

If you believe you have a generalized anxiety disorder that is disrupting your life, fear not because you have already taken the first step to getting help by reading this book. Keep in mind that traditional treatments and alternative therapies are very effective and combining several approaches can make the difference between a life of constant anxiety or one that is fulfilling and symptom-free.

CHAPTER 6

Gripped by Fear

Panic Disorder

Our anxiety does not come from thinking about the future but from trying to control it.

—Kahlil Gibran

S ANDY HAD JUST BOARDED the plane and was placing her carry-on suitcase in the bin above her seat when she heard the flight attendant's panicky voice about a possible bomb threat: everyone had to leave their belongings behind and evacuate the plane as swiftly as possible. Sandy began sweating and could feel her heart pounding, but she did her best to remain calm as she moved quickly to the exit and went down the evacuation slide to the tarmac.

She ran with the others to the terminal and found a bench to sit on but couldn't catch her breath—she was gasping and felt like she was going to die.

The paramedics at the scene said she was hyperventilating, and they had her breathe into a paper bag. Sandy gradually calmed down. They advised her to keep a paper bag with her in the future in case the symptoms returned.

Fortunately, the bomb scare was a false alarm, and no one was hurt. Sandy eventually retrieved her suitcase, hailed a cab, and went straight home, skipping her business trip completely. Still shaken up, Sandy couldn't sleep that night and the next morning she told her husband that she wanted to cancel their upcoming trip to Europe—traveling was too dangerous with all the terrorism going on.

Two days later, Sandy was in the cereal aisle at the supermarket when out of the blue, her heart started pounding again and she had trouble catching her breath. She left her cart full of groceries and ran outside. Fortunately, she had a paper bag in her purse, and breathing into it helped allay her symptoms. The next day she was afraid to go back to the supermarket because she thought it might somehow trigger another terrifying attack.

Sandy worked from home that week and had groceries delivered instead of going to the store. She canceled their weekend dinner plans with friends because she wasn't feeling well. Her husband was understanding, but when Sandy refused to go to a movie because malls weren't safe anymore, he said she was overreacting—they had to go on with their normal lives or the terrorists win. Sandy didn't care and wasn't going out. In fact, she didn't leave the house for more than a month.

*   *   *

Sandy is one of the millions of people who suffer from panic attacks. An estimated one-fourth of the population will experience a spontaneous panic attack at some point in their lifetime. But for Sandy, her panic symptoms became recurrent and led to a secondary fear or phobia of leaving her home or being in a crowd—a condition known as agoraphobia.

Each year, approximately one out of every ten people experiences a panic attack, which can happen without notice or result from a stressful life event. These episodes of sudden onset of intense fear or anxiety are usually short-lived, lasting from about five to twenty minutes. If the attacks recur and interfere with the person's everyday life, a panic disorder may develop. Approximately six million people in the United States suffer from panic disorder, and women are at greater risk than are men.

The underlying cause of panic disorder is not known, but the condition does run in families and often has a genetic component. However, psychological stress, depression, some personality disorders, smoking, and alcohol abuse increase the risk of developing panic disorder.

One explanation for panic disorder is an imbalance in brain chemical messengers or neurotransmitters, which transmit information throughout the brain. As observed in many types of anxiety disorders, levels of such neurotransmitters as serotonin, dopamine, norepinephrine, and gamma-aminobutyric acid (GABA) have been associated with changes in mood and anxiety. Symptoms may be associated with reductions of brain serotonin—the neurotransmitter that regulates mood, sleep, and appetite—or imbalances in dopamine—which influences reward-seeking and attention. Norepinephrine, which modulates the fight-or-flight response to stress, and GABA, the neurotransmitter that balances excitement and relaxation, likely have an impact on panic attacks as well.

When panic occurs, the body's sympathetic nervous system goes into high gear. Essentially the body's fight-or-flight response kicks in—even when no real threat is evident. This panic response worked well for our ancient ancestors when they were attacked by predators, but today, with no predator in sight, panic escalates fearful thinking such as "What's happening to my body?" or "Am I going to die?"

At some point in life, you may well have experienced a panic attack with symptoms similar to what

Sandy endured. If you were fortunate, the symptoms did not recur, but you may be one of the many individuals that suffer from recurrent episodes of panic. Like Sandy, you may have developed fears or phobias related to situations or places where the attacks occurred.

Although people tend to think about panic as a purely psychological problem, it has physiological underpinnings. Fortunately, there are effective treatments for panic attacks, some as simple as breathing into a paper bag. For people with panic attacks or those with associated phobias, talk therapy combined with medication can be very effective.

WHAT IS PANIC DISORDER?

It's normal to experience fear and anxiety from time to time, but full-blown panic attacks are not normal, everyday events. Sometimes these attacks can be predicted when a specific cue or trigger brings on the episode. Sandy's initial attack was triggered by the emergency evacuation from the plane. But very often, panic attacks happen unexpectedly and may occur almost anywhere or any time. The individual may be completely relaxed when such an unexpected attack suddenly occur, seemingly without an apparent external cue (e.g., scary event) or internal cue (e.g., fear thought) triggering it.

DO YOU HAVE PANIC DISORDER?

Consider whether you have experienced attacks of intense fear or dread that happen out of the blue. If these attacks were accompanied by several of the following symptoms, then panic disorder may be the source of your unease.

- ☐ pounding heart
- ☐ sweating
- ☐ shakiness
- ☐ dizziness
- ☐ chills or sensations of heat
- ☐ shortness of breath
- ☐ feeling like you're choking
- ☐ fear of going crazy or dying
- ☐ feelings of unreality or being detached from yourself

Because of his concerns about Sandy's behavior since the incident on the airplane, her husband talked her into meeting with a psychiatrist. She was initially reluctant but eventually agreed to see someone her internist recommended. At her first visit, Sandy described her chronic worry about experiencing further attacks and how she often thought about the terror she felt when evacuating from the plane. She talked about how her daily life had changed because she was now avoiding crowds and public

DIAGNOSTIC FEATURES OF PANIC DISORDER

- The features include recurring, unexpected, and abrupt onset of attacks involving feelings of intense fear or discomfort that peak within minutes. These panic attacks include four or more of the following:
  - pounding heart or rapid heart rate
  - sweating
  - shaking, trembling
  - shortness of breath or feeling smothered
  - feelings of choking
  - chest discomfort or pain
  - nausea or upset stomach
  - sensations of heat or chills
  - dizziness or light-headedness
  - sensations of numbness or tingling
  - feeling unreal or detached from oneself
  - fear of dying
  - fear of going crazy

- At least one of these attacks has been followed by a month of persistent worry about future attacks or maladaptive behavior associated with the attacks or both.

- The attacks are not associated with a medical condition or substance abuse.

places. It seemed like the only place she felt relaxed was at home, and it was tough for her just to come see the doctor. In fact, when Sandy first left the house, she felt her heart start racing, and she couldn't catch her breath, but breathing into the bag she now kept in her purse helped calm her down.

When people hyperventilate, they are exhaling too much carbon dioxide. Breathing into a bag or holding one's breath for a short time will increase the body's carbon dioxide levels, which helps calm them down. If patients continue to hyperventilate, they may develop sensations of tingling in their extremities, which are known as paresthesias that are caused by elevated blood levels of carbon dioxide. Sandy clearly had the diagnostic features of panic disorder as described in the American Psychiatric Association's Diagnostic and Statistical Manual of Mental Disorders.

Sandy developed a secondary anxiety disorder that is often associated with panic attacks. She began to fear places that she associated with the attacks, such as the supermarket or eventually anywhere outside her home. This is often described as panic attacks with secondary agoraphobia, which afflicts about one out of every three patients with panic attacks. Such patients' symptoms often begin when they experience physical and emotional symptoms of panic that can seem to come from nowhere and end abruptly. For some patients like Sandy, a particular event, like a terrorist scare, can trigger the initial panic attack. A physical condition may bring on the symptoms, such as a heart flutter from a mitral valve prolapse. Sometimes the patient has a genetic predisposition to panic. For instance, Sandy had a family history of anxiety on her mother's side.

In her mind, Sandy associated the location of the initial attack as its cause, so she avoided the airport and other crowded places that reminded her of the initial attack. This learned response then developed into a phobia for these places, and over time, her movements became more and more restricted. Eventually, patients like Sandy who develop full-blown agoraphobia can become housebound.

ACCURATE DIAGNOSIS

Many patients with panic attacks are so focused on avoiding future attacks that they fail to obtain a proper diagnosis. Because many of the symptoms of panic are physical, patients may obtain multiple medical consultations searching for an underlying physical condition as the cause, unaware that their symptoms are the result of a psychiatric disorder.

This is unfortunate since panic disorder can have a negative impact on a person's everyday life and well-being. Patients like Sandy often lose time from work and have trouble functioning normally. Some patients become so desperate to end their discomfort that they consider suicide as an option. Patients with panic disorder have a higher rate of other medical illnesses, particularly heart disease. Despite what the patient may believe, chest pain that develops during the panic attack is usually not due to a heart problem.

MEDICAL CONDITIONS OFTEN PRESENT IN PANIC DISORDER PATIENTS

- allergies
- cancer
- cardiac disease
- chronic pain
- irritable bowel syndrome
- migraine
- mitral valve prolapse (bulging heart valve)
- respiratory disease
- thyroid disease
- vestibular (inner ear) disorder

To obtain an accurate diagnosis, the doctor will inquire about details of the recent symptoms as well as past history of psychiatric and medical conditions.

These can include any use of alcohol or drugs, prescribed and over-the-counter medications, and other
substances such as caffeine that can worsen symptoms. Major life events, certain occupations (e.g.,
military service), and a family history of similar disorders may also increase risk for panic and guide the
doctor toward an accurate diagnosis. The doctor may
also draw blood to test for thyroid abnormalities or
other medical conditions that could contribute to
symptoms.

CONVENTIONAL THERAPIES FOR PANIC DISORDER

Combining drug treatment with psychotherapy is
usually the most effective strategy for treating panic
disorder. If symptoms are recurrent, medication
treatment is a first-line intervention for panic disorder. Several drugs have been shown to be effective, including antidepressant medicines such as the
selective serotonin reuptake inhibitors (SSRIs; e.g.,
Prozac, Zoloft), serotonin-norepinephrine reuptake
inhibitors (SNRIs; e.g., Cymbalta, Effexor), and tricyclic antidepressants (e.g., Pamelor, Tofranil). Antianxiety medicines such as benzodiazepines also
reduce symptoms in severe cases. Unfortunately,
anywhere from 20 to 60 percent of panic disorder
patients in clinical trials do not respond adequately
to their initial medication treatment.

MEDICATIONS FOR TREATMENT
OF PANIC ATTACKS

- *Antidepressants* include the following:
  - ○ Selective serotonin reuptake inhibitors (SSRIs) and serotonin norepinephrine reuptake inhibitor (SNRIs) are first-line treatments and may take weeks or months to become effective. Tricyclic antidepressants are also effective in many cases. Monoamine oxidase inhibitors (MAOIs) are effective but require dietary restrictions to avoid serious side effects. Examples include citalopram (Celexa), fluvoxamine (Luvox), paroxetine (Paxil), imipramine (Tofranil), venlafaxine (Effexor), and phenelzine (Nardil).

- *Minor tranquilizers or benzodiazepines* can help reduce the anxiety and feelings of fear associated with panic. They can become habit-forming, however, and they may cause side effects when used with alcohol. These medicines need to be used with caution and only when symptoms are incapacitating. Examples include alprazolam (Xanax), clonazepam (Klonopin), diazepam (Valium), and lorazepam (Ativan).

A recent meta-analysis of previous clinical trials for panic disorder identified three important findings: longer duration of illness was associated with poorer outcomes, older age was associated with more

---

DID YOU KNOW?

- Some people get panic attacks while sound asleep. These episodes are similar to usual panic attacks during the day and may include shortness of breath and chest pain.

- Although people naturally try to avoid situations they believe will cause their attacks, such avoidance behavior actually increases fearfulness and restricts daily functioning.

- About one in every four patients who present to their doctor with chest pain actually has panic disorder.

---

dropouts from treatment, and longer duration of treatment led to higher rates of treatment success. The bottom line is that individuals with panic disorder need to be patient because the initial medication might not work. It may need to be switched to another one from either the same class or a different class of medication, or it could take weeks or months to become effective. It is important to work closely with your doctor so your medication treatment can be personalized for optimal effectiveness.

Despite its dramatic and debilitating consequences, panic disorder and agoraphobia respond well to antidepressants and cognitive behavioral therapy (CBT), such as desensitization psychotherapy. The medication helps eliminate the panic attacks and the therapy helps the patient gradually overcome their phobia of the outside world.

Psychotherapy can also be effective in reducing panic symptoms. Panic-focused CBT, through individual or group sessions, can be delivered weekly and can reduce symptoms within months. Many patients find psychodynamic psychotherapy useful in helping them avoid maladaptive behaviors that complicate their symptoms and functioning. Other approaches, such as family therapy and supportive psychotherapy, can help patients deal with interpersonal and other psychological stressors that contribute to symptoms.

Patients with accompanying agoraphobia often benefit from desensitization psychotherapy, which gradually teaches patients to remain calm in perceived stressful situations. Patients make lists of places and situations that trigger their fear reaction and then rank those different situations according to the degree of anxiety experienced with each. The therapist begins with the least disturbing scenario and teaches the patient relaxation exercises to use in order to tolerate these anxiety-provoking situations.

Numerous positive randomized controlled trials have demonstrated the effectiveness of individual or group CBT for panic disorder. Desensitization or exposure therapy has also been shown to be effective in several investigations.

Sandy responded well to an antidepressant medication and desensitization therapy. Over time, she became more comfortable leaving the house and going out to public places. She gradually got back to living normally, and after six months of treatment, Sandy finally took that vacation in Europe with her husband.

ALTERNATIVE STRATEGIES FOR PANIC

Some clinicians have used psychodynamic therapy in patients with panic disorder, but systematic evidence for its effectiveness is limited. One controlled study did show that panic-focused psychodynamic psychotherapy was effective in relieving symptoms.

Other treatments, such as eye movement desensitization and reprocessing, have not been formally tested for panic disorder or have been shown to be ineffective or less effective than standard treatments like CBT. Even without systematic data demonstrating effectiveness, many clinicians recommend a variety of stress-reducing interventions that can lower anxiety levels and thus reduce symptoms associated with panic attacks and related feelings of fear as well as associated phobias. Some herbal remedies that help calm people may also temporarily reduce symptoms in some patients, although systematic studies of these in panic disorder are limited. Many alternative panic disorder interventions have been used successfully to augment the benefits of conventional treatments.

ALTERNATIVE PANIC DISORDER INTERVENTIONS

- *dietary and herbal supplements*
  - inositol, kava, l-lysine/l-arginine combination
- *biofeedback and neurofeedback*
- *bodywork*
  - massage, acupuncture, acupressure
- *other approaches*
  - exercise, meditation, yoga, music, pets, volunteering

Studies have shown that regular exercise can reduce symptoms of anxiety, and many patients with panic symptoms report feeling better when they remain physically active. Proper nutrition may also reduce the frequency and degree of symptoms. Excessive amounts of caffeine, alcohol, or even monosodium glutamate (MSG) may increase symptoms of anxiety and worsen panic attacks.

Knowledge of the condition and its effective treatments is comforting for many patients who no longer have to fear that they are losing control. Many feel reassured when they understand that brain changes are driving their symptoms and that those symptoms will pass if they wait them out.

CHAPTER 7

Shy to a Fault

Social Anxiety

Happiness is having a large, loving, caring, close-knit family in another city.

—George Burns

FOR AS LONG AS Larry could remember, he had been extremely shy. It seemed to get worse when he was thirteen and entered puberty. His voice suddenly got deeper and would constantly crack—he couldn't control it—and it made him more self-conscious. Even calling somebody on the phone became a major challenge for him.

Larry's anxieties grew worse when the other boys his age became interested in girls and started spending time with them. Larry got nervous even thinking about talking to a girl on his own. His palms would sweat, and he was convinced that everyone would notice how anxious he was.

Because Larry was uncomfortable making eye contact with both peers and adults, he got in the habit of averting his eyes when he first met someone. This discomfort would ease somewhat when he got to know someone better, but all his worries about social encounters made it hard for him to meet new people in the first place.

Despite his symptoms, Larry was able to graduate from college and obtain a degree in computer science. He had always been good at math and spent a lot of time playing video games growing up. Larry landed a job as a computer programmer, which was perfect for him since it didn't require a lot of people skills.

Through the years, Larry's parents tried to get him to see a therapist for help with his symptoms, but Larry felt so much shame about his shyness that he was too embarrassed to talk about it, even with a professional. Besides, he was in his midtwenties, had a full-time job, and paid for his own apartment so he didn't think he needed any therapy. Although Larry tried to convince himself that he had overcome his disability, deep down he knew he was different from other people, and he felt lonely and isolated. He seldom dated and spent most of his free time at home playing video games. He often had trouble sleeping at night, and sometimes Larry wondered if he would be better off dead—then his parents wouldn't have to worry about him so much.

*   *   *

Although Larry's situation sounds extreme, it is more commonplace than you may imagine. He suffered from social anxiety disorder, which is the most common form of anxiety disorder. Over a twelve-month period, the prevalence of social anxiety disorder in the United States is 7 percent. It occurs about twice as often in women and girls than in men and boys.

For Larry and other people who suffer from social anxiety disorder, it has a tremendous negative impact on their daily lives. It interferes with a person's ability to succeed in school and work and clearly impairs relationships, making it difficult to date, get married, and remain married. Patients also have a higher risk of depression and substance abuse.

Larry was fortunate that he had some success in school and work, but he probably would have done much better had he received proper treatment for his disorder. His insomnia, loneliness, and passive thoughts of dying probably indicated that he was also suffering from a major depression—another mental disorder that responds well to treatment. His depression was a reaction to the impairment he experienced from his social anxiety.

DO YOU HAVE SOCIAL ANXIETY DISORDER?

People with social anxiety disorder experience intense anxiety and fear of social situations. Check off any of the following situations that might make you feel fear or anxiety. If you check off four or more, you may be experiencing symptoms of social anxiety.

☐   shopping alone at the mall

☐   asking a salesperson for help

☐   greeting someone who is an authority figure

☐   singing at a karaoke bar

☐   going on a job interview

☐   saying hello to a stranger

☐   answering the phone without seeing who is calling

☐   interrupting someone during a conversation

☐   talking when there's a lull in a conversation

☐   speaking to a group of four or more people

WHAT IS SOCIAL ANXIETY DISORDER?

People with social anxiety dread social situations involving interactions with other people. These individuals are afraid of being evaluated or judged by others, and their symptoms impact nearly every aspect of their life. Patients with social anxiety usually come off as quiet, shy, inhibited, nervous, and aloof, and although they want to make friends and be included in groups, their anxiety and fear hold them back. The disorder is chronic, and many patients are reluctant to undergo any type of treatment.

A variety of situations will trigger symptoms, such as being introduced to new people, being teased, or being the center of attention. Public speaking is usually a major trigger for symptoms, as is dealing with authority figures or making direct eye contact with other people. Even swallowing, shaking hands, or making a phone call can bring on symptoms. Conversations with others, encountering unfamiliar people, and eating or drinking in public places are common triggers.

The symptoms of social anxiety disorder usually develop in childhood or adolescence: 75 percent of cases have their onset between the ages of eight and fifteen years old. Sometimes it begins after a stressful or humiliating experience, such as being bullied or having a panic attack in public, or the symptoms may develop slowly without a clear precipitating event.

DIAGNOSING SOCIAL ANXIETY

Many individuals with social anxiety disorder live with it for years or even decades without seeking help so they are unaware of their diagnosis and the possibility of receiving effective treatments that are available. Mild social anxiety is common in nearly everyone—at some point in life almost all of us experience fear of public speaking or anxiety in certain social situations, but the degree of the symptoms and their duration don't impair our lives to the extent that they do in patients with the disorder.

Patients with social anxiety disorder need to be differentiated from those experiencing other related mental health conditions. Normal shyness is a common personality trait and doesn't disrupt the individual's life. In fact, in some societies, shyness is perceived as an asset. Only about 10 percent of people who are shy actually have social anxiety disorder.

People with agoraphobia or fear of crowds and public places sometimes experience fright and anxiety in social situations because they are worried that they may not be able to escape if they develop a panic attack. By contrast, those with social anxiety fear the scrutiny of other people.

Socially anxious patients may experience panic attacks because they are scared that others will evaluate them in a negative way, whereas those with panic disorder fear their actual panic attacks. Patients with generalized anxiety disorder often have social worries, but their focus of concern is more about relationships in general rather than scrutiny from others.

Many patients with social anxiety disorder suffer from other psychiatric disorders as well, including

DIAGNOSTIC FEATURES OF
SOCIAL ANXIETY DISORDER

Specific diagnostic criteria have been described in the American Psychiatric Association's Diagnostic and Statistical Manual of Mental Disorders and include the following features:

- The individual experiences prominent fear or anxiety triggered by social situations that induce a perception of being scrutinized by others.

- There is fear that the display of anxiety symptoms will lead to humiliation, rejection, or embarrassment or somehow offend others.

- The same social situations almost always provoke the symptoms.

- The individual avoids the anxiety-provoking situations or endures them with intense fear or anxiety.

- The fear and anxiety are out of proportion to the actual threat.

- The symptoms have persisted for at least six months.

- The symptoms and avoiding them disrupts social, occupational, or other areas of function.

substance abuse, major depression, and bipolar disorder. Usually the social anxiety precedes the development of the other disorder. In Larry's case, he became depressed because of the isolation he experienced from his social anxiety. Other patients will self-medicate with drugs and develop alcohol or substance abuse disorders.

CONVENTIONAL THERAPIES FOR SOCIAL ANXIETY DISORDER

Individuals who suffer from social anxiety disorder are generally aware of the fact that their anxiety symptoms are irrational, but their uncomfortable thoughts and feelings of anxiety don't go away on their own. However, therapeutic interventions have been shown to be effective and to even alter the brain's structure and neural pathways.

Many studies have shown that cognitive behavioral therapy (CBT) for social anxiety is remarkably effective and can be delivered as one-on-one individual treatment, group therapy, or even online. This form of therapy helps patients alter their thoughts, beliefs, and feelings as well as their behaviors.

Although medications can reduce symptoms of social anxiety, some research indicates that CBT can be more effective than certain antidepressant medications. Dr. Hans Nordahl and colleagues of St. Olav's University Hospital in Norway compared the efficacy of the selective serotonin reuptake inhibitor (SSRI) paroxetine, CBT, and the combination of both medication and therapy in more than one hundred

---

THERAPY FOR SOCIAL ANXIETY
DISORDER CHANGES THE BRAIN

A group of Swedish investigators performed magnetic resonance imaging (MRI) scans on patients with social anxiety disorder before and after just nine weeks of internet-delivered cognitive behavioral therapy (CBT). They found that the CBT altered both brain volume and activity in the amygdala, one of the brain's most important emotional control centers. The more that patients improved from the therapy, the smaller the volume in the amygdala. Moreover, the smaller the amygdala, the less neural activity was observed in that brain region. Other studies using positron emission tomography (PET) scans have demonstrated reduced neural activity in the amygdala as well as the hippocampal memory center in social anxiety disorder patients treated with either CBT or antidepressant medication.

---

volunteers with social anxiety disorder. The volunteers received either paroxetine, CBT, paroxetine plus CBT, or placebo. The treatment lasted for twenty-six weeks, and at the end of the treatment period and after twelve months of follow-up, participants who had received CBT improved significantly and maintained benefits better than those who received placebo or paroxetine alone. Nearly 70 percent of the research subjects receiving CBT recovered compared with only 40 percent of those receiving combination therapy, 24 percent receiving paroxetine alone, and 4 percent receiving placebo.

In patients with social anxiety disorder, CBT can help them recognize what triggers their social anxiety and revise their distorted thoughts and beliefs regarding the social situations they fear. This allows the patient to then adopt alternative and more realistic thoughts and beliefs about their anxiety triggers and develop more adaptive behaviors to improve their lives.

Most of the time, CBT for social anxiety can be administered successfully once per week for sixteen weeks. The effectiveness of CBT for social anxiety appears to be comparable whether it is done on an individual basis or in group settings.

Other forms of therapy have been shown to be effective as well, including social skills training, relaxation exercises, and exposure therapy alone or in combination with behavioral therapy. Group CBT is effective in targeting specific symptoms such as public speaking anxiety.

Exposure therapy, in which the patient is gradually exposed to the social situations that trigger their anxiety, is often used in psychotherapy for social anxiety disorder. In the therapist's office, the patient imagines an anxiety-provoking situation, and the therapist helps comfort the patient to gradually become less anxious in the imagined situation. As the patient's confidence grows, it is then possible to experience those once-feared situations in the real world. Sometimes the therapist will accompany the patient outside the office to help build the patient's confidence in various scenarios.

Acceptance and Commitment Therapy (ACT) is a form of CBT that shows some promise in treating social anxiety disorder. This intervention involves working to create a rich and meaningful life while accepting the pain that may accompany it. It differs from traditional CBT in that it teaches the patient to accept and deal with their negative thoughts rather than to reduce them.

TREATMENTS FOR SOCIAL ANXIETY DISORDER

- cognitive behavioral therapy

- exposure therapy

- social skills training

- acceptance and commitment therapy (ACT)

- relaxation training

- antidepressant medications (e.g., paroxetine [Paxil], sertraline [Zoloft], fluoxetine [Prozac], venlafaxine [Effexor])

- antianxiety medications (e.g., lorazepam [Ativan], alprazolam [Xanax])

Medication may be helpful in reducing symptoms of social anxiety but is not always necessary. Anti-anxiety agents, certain antidepressants, and other medications have been shown to reduce symptoms.

The SSRI antidepressants have been shown to provide benefits in reducing anxiety. Commonly used SSRIs for social anxiety include paroxetine (Paxil), sertraline (Zoloft), escitalopram (Lexapro), citalopram (Celexa), and fluoxetine (Prozac). Serotonin and norepinephrine reuptake inhibitors (SNRIs) such as venlafaxine (Effexor) also have been used to treat social anxiety. It can take about six to eight weeks for these antidepressant medicines to have an effect on symptoms.

Benzodiazepines (e.g., lorazepam [Ativan], alprazolam [Xanax]) have an immediate effect on symptoms but may cause sedation and cognitive side effects. They also can become habit-forming, so they should be used with caution.

Beta-blockers (e.g., propranolol [Inderal], atenolol [Tenormin]) block the flow of epinephrine (also known as adrenaline), which increases in the brain during anxiety episodes. Beta-blockers have short-term effects and alleviate anxiety associated with performance or public speaking.

For patients who are willing to pursue conventional therapies for social anxiety, the prognosis is quite good. Those completing a course of CBT have remarkably high success rates. A key to success, of course, is the patient's ability to continue using the therapeutic strategies that have been shown to be effective.

DID YOU KNOW?

- It is extremely rare for someone to develop symptoms of social anxiety disorder for the first time after age twenty-five.

- Women are twice as likely to suffer from social anxiety disorder as are men.

- Most people with social anxiety disorder never receive proper treatment even though treatments have been shown to be highly effective.

- Approximately 20 percent of people with social anxiety disorder receive public assistance or welfare compared to about 10 percent of the general population.

ALTERNATIVE AND SELF-HELP STRATEGIES FOR SOCIAL ANXIETY

Many of the interventions that reduce social anxiety can be done without a therapist. For example, CBT and relaxation techniques are available online and have been shown to be effective.

Changes in dietary habits can help many forms of anxiety, including social anxiety. People who consume a Mediterranean-style diet consisting of vegetables, fruit, lean meat, fish, and whole grains have a lower risk of anxiety disorders in general according to population-based studies. By contrast, those who eat a "Western diet" that includes processed meats, pizza, chocolates, sweets, soft drinks, margarine, French fries, beer, coffee, cake, and ice cream have greater risks for anxiety symptoms. Other dietary adjustments can help reduce symptoms, such as decreasing caffeine consumption and use of alcohol in excess. Occasionally, food allergies can contribute to anxiety symptoms so making sure the patient does not have specific food allergies may be indicated in some cases.

Physical exercise can reduce symptoms of depression as well as anxiety, although systematic research specifically linking relief of social anxiety disorder symptoms and exercise is limited. However, research has demonstrated an association between lack of physical activity and social anxiety symptoms, and interventions such as home-based walking programs and a combination of group CBT with exercise have been effective.

People who report symptoms of insomnia also show a greater severity of social anxiety disorder. Poor quality of sleep has been demonstrated to reduce the effectiveness of social anxiety treatments.

Mindfulness therapies can also help patients alter their perception of negative thoughts, so they simply view them as thoughts and words that come and go and have minimal value. Changing this perception can help decrease the power of those thoughts in triggering a fear or anxiety reaction.

A variety of herbal supplements have been used to treat social anxiety, including chamomile, kava, winter cherry, valerian root, St. John's wort, passion-flower, and others. Keep in mind that little scientific evidence supports the effectiveness of these supplements for symptoms of social anxiety.

CHAPTER 8

Germs, Bugs, and Heights, Oh My

Phobias

*A new study shows that having a
severe phobia can hasten aging. But
what if my greatest fear is aging?*
—Stephen Colbert

NANCY STILL RECALLED THE incident from her childhood in vivid detail. She was eleven years old
and all the kids were playing with the neighbor's new
German Shepard. Nancy reached out to pet the dog,
but it got spooked and lunged at her face.

She must have blacked out because the next thing
Nancy remembered was being in the emergency
room and noticing the blood all over her blouse. Her
lip was numb, and she could feel the stitches with her
tongue.

Over the next few months, the scar healed well, but ever since that day, Nancy was afraid of dogs. She managed to avoid them over the years, even as her own kids grew up, which wasn't easy because so many of their friends had dogs. Nancy would only visit pet owners if they put their dogs outside, and if she saw a dog walking toward her on the street, Nancy would get out of the way and wait until it passed.

If she let her guard down and happened to find herself near a dog—big or small—Nancy's heart would pound, and she would feel faint. Just thinking about that day the dog bit her could bring on anxiety symptoms. Interestingly, spiders, snakes, or any other kind of animal didn't seem to bother her at all.

When Nancy's daughter Gayle was home from college one winter break, she found a lost puppy on the street and brought it home. Gayle begged her mother to let her keep it until she could find the owner. She promised Nancy that she would keep the puppy in a crate in the laundry room at all times. Nancy was skeptical, but she finally gave in—Gayle could be so persistent.

The problem was that the puppy cried all night, and Nancy couldn't stand it. She turned on the light in the laundry room and the puppy was so happy to see her he stopped crying, jumped up and down, and tried to lick her through the cage. Nancy stayed there a few minutes, but when she left the room, the pup immediately started crying again. Nancy didn't want the whole family to be woken up, so she brought in a chair and sat in the laundry room until the puppy fell asleep.

The same thing happened the next few nights. Nancy would come down to the laundry room, and the happy puppy would stop crying and try to lick her. He was so cute and little that eventually Nancy felt comfortable enough to sit on the floor next to the crate. With her anxiety better controlled, Nancy eventually built up the nerve to let the caged pup lick her fingers.

When Gayle's attempts to find the owner failed, she begged Nancy to keep the puppy. Nancy was tempted, but she was concerned that her anxiety symptoms would return. She searched "dog phobias" on the internet and learned that there were effective treatments. She decided to reach out to her doctor for a therapist referral.

* * *

Nancy suffered from a *specific phobia*, or a dispro-portionate fear of a particular object or situation that limited her functioning. This type of restrictive fear is one of the most common forms of anxiety disor-der and affects one out of every eight people at some time in their life.

Fear of dogs is also known as *cynophobia* and is one of the most prevalent animal phobias, along with fear of snakes and spiders. Because dogs are so common in our society, it's more difficult to avoid them than other types of animals, making cynophobia a particularly stressful phobia. Like Nancy, most people with such phobias are either too embarrassed to seek treatment or unaware that effective therapies are available.

TOP TEN SPECIFIC PHOBIAS

Phobia Name	Feared Object or Situation
Acrophobia	Heights
Astraphobia	Storms
Claustrophobia	Enclosed spaces
Cynophobia	Dogs
Entomophobia	Insects
Ophidiophobia	Snakes
Pteromerhanophobia	Flying
Social phobia	People
Trypanophobia	Needles

Phobic symptoms usually begin in early childhood and in most cases develop before ten years of age. Epidemiological studies indicate that over any twelve-month period, approximately 7 to 9 percent of people in the United States experience a specific phobia. Older adults experience a slightly lower rate—in the range of 3 to 5 percent—compared with younger adults. Women are twice as likely to suffer from phobias as are men. The rates of specific phobic disorder are a bit lower in Asia, Africa, and Latin America, ranging between 2 and 4 percent.

Even though specific phobias are less frequent in older adults than younger adults, they are still relatively common. Many times, phobias in older individuals occur in the presence of chronic medical concerns, such as heart or lung disease. Older adults are also more likely to attribute their anxiety symptoms to a physical condition.

Any negative experience can trigger a phobia, but genetics contribute to an individual's risk as well. If you have a parent or sibling with a phobic disorder, your risk is increased. Changes in brain functioning also play a role in developing specific phobias.

RECOGNIZING PHOBIAS

Any extreme or irrational fear reaction to a situation or object may be a phobia. People with phobias often feel a profound sense of dread or panic if they encounter the feared object or situation. Phobias differ from general anxiety disorders in that the symptoms are linked to a specific stimulus.

Some people are afraid of heights or confined spaces; others fear flying, while others experience intense anxiety when exposed to a particular animal or a needle for a blood draw. In Nancy's case, she only had a specific phobia of dogs and did not fear other

SPECIFIC PHOBIAS AND YOUR BRAIN

Neuroscientists have used a variety of brain scanning methods to understand how the brain functions in people with specific phobias. A comprehensive scientific review of these various studies concluded that compared with control subjects without phobias, specific-phobia patients exposed to phobia-related situations show greater neural activation in several brain regions that control relevant mental functions including the following:

Brain Region	Function
Amygdala	Perceiving fear and emotion
Anterior cingulate cortex	Decision-making and emotional regulation
Insula	Emotional context for sensory experience
Orbitofrontal cortex	Cognitive processing of decision-making
Prefrontal cortex	Complex behavior and decision-making

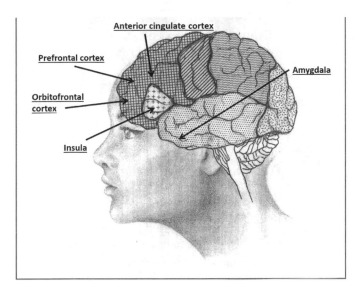

situations or objects. However, many phobic individuals do suffer from multiple phobias.

The feelings of fear or anxiety that arise from specific phobic disorders definitely differ from the normal and transient fears that nearly everyone experiences from time to time. Sometimes the fearful episodes of a phobia even take the form of a full panic attack.

Phobias can range from being annoying to severely disabling. These kinds of fearful reactions can interfere with many aspects of life, impairing the patient's educational, professional, and personal functions. A typical feature of a specific phobia is that the individual goes to great lengths to avoid the anxiety-provoking situation or object. This was certainly true in Nancy's case. Although her phobia restricted

DIAGNOSTIC FEATURES OF A
SPECIFIC PHOBIC DISORDER

The American Psychiatric Association's Diagnostic Manual of Mental Disorders includes the following criteria for a diagnosis of a specific phobia:

- There is intense fear or anxiety related to a specific object or situation.

- The feared object or situation nearly always induces immediate fear or anxiety.

- The individual actively avoids the feared object or situation or is forced to endure the intense fear or anxiety that arises.

- The fear or anxiety is out of proportion to the real danger that the specific object or situation might pose.

- The fear, anxiety, or avoidance usually persists six months or more.

- The fear, anxiety, or avoidance leads to significant distress or impairment in social, occupational, or other areas of functioning.

- The disturbance cannot be explained by another mental disorder.

her in many situations, she was still able to continue functioning in other areas of her life.

Often, specific phobias develop after a particular traumatic event: sometimes an individual gets stuck in an elevator; other times, as with Nancy, the person is attacked by an animal. Still other individuals have no recall of any particular precipitating event.

People with a neurotic personality style are at greater risk of developing specific phobias. An overprotective parent during childhood or a loss of a parent through divorce or death also predisposes a child to phobias. Genetic factors increase risk: someone with a parent or sibling with a specific phobia has a greater risk of developing a phobia.

Some people suffer from social anxiety disorder, which is also known as social phobia. These individuals have a marked fear or anxiety about social situations where they feel exposed to possible scrutiny by others. Sometimes they are afraid of having conversations or meeting unfamiliar people. Others with social phobias feel anxiety if they are observed eating or drinking or giving a speech in public. Any situation that could potentially make the individual feel negatively evaluated, humiliated, embarrassed, or rejected may trigger the symptoms.

Another form of phobia, agoraphobia, can develop in individuals who suffer from panic attacks. Agoraphobia actually means "fear of open spaces," and these individuals are often frightened of venturing outside their homes. They may also experience anxiety when in confined or crowded spaces.

DIAGNOSTIC FEATURES OF AGORAPHOBIA

The American Psychiatric Association's Diagnostic Manual of Mental Disorders includes the following criteria for a diagnosis of agoraphobia:

- There is intense fear or anxiety about two or more of the following situations:
  - using automobiles, buses, trains, planes, or other public transportation
  - being in parking lots, marketplaces, bridges, or other open spaces
  - being in shops, theaters, cinemas, or other enclosed spaces
  - standing in line or being in a crowd
  - being outside of the home alone

- The person fears or avoids such situations because it might be difficult for them to escape or get help if they develop panic or other embarrassing symptoms.

- The feared and avoided situation nearly always provokes the symptoms.

- The individual actively avoids these situations or requires someone to be with them to avoid the symptoms.

- The fear or anxiety is out of proportion to the real danger of the feared situation or object.

- The symptoms usually persist six months or more.

- The disturbance cannot be explained by another mental disorder.

CONVENTIONAL THERAPIES FOR PHOBIC DISORDER

For specific phobias like Nancy's fear of dogs, exposure therapy is very effective. Multiple controlled clinical trials have demonstrated its efficacy—one investigation even showed 90 percent effectiveness that was sustained after several years of follow-up. It turns out that understanding the cause of a phobia is not as important as focusing on how to deal with the avoidance behavior that patients develop over time. For people suffering from multiple phobias, the therapy usually involves focusing on one phobia at a time.

Exposure therapy helps patients face their anxieties through exercises that gradually expose them to the anxiety-provoking situation or object. With gradual exposure therapy, the patient creates a hierarchy of feared scenarios and then begins with exposure to the least frightening one. As their confidence builds, patients then move on to the next most frightening experience. They continue the process until they eventually become desensitized to their fears.

On her own, Nancy gradually exposed herself to the caged puppy and began to gain control over her fears. Her doctor referred her to a cognitive behavioral therapist who very gradually helped Nancy approach a dog while he coached her on ways to deal with her anxiety. Nancy learned relaxation exercises and continued with the exposure therapy in a systematic way until she was comfortable keeping the puppy. After several months of therapy, Nancy began to feel more at ease around other dogs. With the help of her therapist, she learned that dogs, as well as the anxiety they caused her, were not as dangerous as she had imagined.

DID YOU KNOW?

- *Nomophobia* is the fear of losing your mobile phone or its signal.

- William Shakespeare and Alexander the Great were *ailurophobes*–they feared cats.

Exposure therapy, a form of cognitive behavioral therapy (CBT), and other elements of CBT can be effective in treating phobias. This usually involves combining exposure therapy with strategies to help the patient learn more effective ways to view and cope with the feared object or situation. By learning to understand their fears and body sensations, patients can reduce the negative impact that the disorder has on their lives.

Although exposure therapy is usually effective in treating specific phobias, sometimes, medications such as beta-blockers or benzodiazepines can further decrease the anxiety and panic symptoms patients experience when exposed to their feared object or situation. Medications can be helpful for patients suffering from fear of flying, public speaking, or coping with fear of enclosed spaces such as MRI scanners; however, it's best to limit the use of medications to the initial treatment period.

When people are experiencing their anxiety, they usually feel physical symptoms, including a pounding heart (palpitations), rapid heart rate, shaking voice, and excess perspiration. The stress hormone adrenaline causes these physical symptoms, and medicines known as beta-blockers can reduce anxiety by interrupting the stimulating effects of adrenaline. Sedating medications called benzodiazepines can also help relax the patient but should be used cautiously because they can be addictive.

TREATMENTS FOR PHOBIC DISORDERS

- **psychotherapy**
  - **exposure therapy**
  - **cognitive behavioral therapy**
- **medication**
  - **beta-blockers**
  - **sedatives**

Patients with agoraphobia secondary to panic attacks also benefit from exposure therapy and other forms of CBT. Their panic attacks, however, often need to be treated using an SSRI antidepressant.

SELF-HELP AND ALTERNATIVE STRATEGIES FOR PHOBIC DISORDERS

Many of the alternative and self-help strategies that reduce anxiety associated with panic attacks are also helpful for patients suffering from phobias. Mindfulness strategies can help patients better tolerate their anxiety symptoms and reduce their avoidance behaviors. Deep breathing, progressive muscle relaxation, yoga, or related techniques also may reduce stress and help patients cope with their symptoms. Numerous studies have shown that physical exercise can improve mood and reduce anxiety symptoms as well.

Although the natural response to fearful stimuli is to avoid them, patients can reduce avoidance behavior by attempting to stay near to feared situations as long and as often as they can rather than avoid them completely. Engaging the support of family, friends, and trained therapists can also help reduce avoidance behavior.

Joining a self-help or support group can help patients connect with others who understand the condition and can provide both practical and emotional

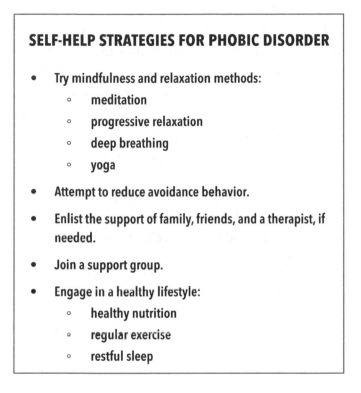

SELF-HELP STRATEGIES FOR PHOBIC DISORDER

- Try mindfulness and relaxation methods:
    - meditation
    - progressive relaxation
    - deep breathing
    - yoga
- Attempt to reduce avoidance behavior.
- Enlist the support of family, friends, and a therapist, if needed.
- Join a support group.
- Engage in a healthy lifestyle:
    - healthy nutrition
    - regular exercise
    - restful sleep

support. Engaging in other positive lifestyle habits that boost brain health may also improve the patient's level of functioning. Consuming a healthy diet, getting enough rest, and avoiding excess caffeine may further help patients cope with phobias.

Complementary medicines and therapies also have been used for phobic disorder. Some herbal medicines like kava have demonstrated beneficial effects. Limited data support the use of acupuncture, tai chi, and homeopathy for treating phobic disorders.

In recent years, many clinical investigations have utilized virtual reality technologies to enhance the effectiveness of exposure therapy. For example, a recent study used a computer game involving various traffic situations that simulated driving scenarios. The investigators found that volunteers using this technology experienced a reduction in anxiety symptoms suggesting the utility of this approach for specific phobias. Virtual reality exposure therapy has also shown initial success for dental phobias, fear of storms, and several other specific phobias.

CHAPTER 9

Can't Stop Those Thoughts

Obsessive-Compulsive Disorder

> *I have CDO. It's like OCD but all the*
> *letters are in alphabetical order.*
> —Venice Beach, California, T-shirt

ELISE AND JIM HAD been together since high school, and a month after they graduated from college they got married and moved in together. They got along really well, although they both had to learn to live with each other's idiosyncrasies. Elise often described herself as a "nitpicker"—she liked everything in its place and always made sure the house was spotless and uncluttered. She claimed to have inherited this from her "clean-freak" mother, and although Jim tolerated Elise's need for cleanliness, it seemed to get worse and more irritating every year. He couldn't place a glass on a table without Elise swooping in with a coaster. If he left a jacket on the back of a chair, she rushed it to the closet and scolded him to be more thoughtful.

This year was especially stressful because Elise's mother was coming to stay for a few weeks, and Elise insisted that Jim help her keep the house immaculate at all times. Jim told her that she was overdoing it, but Elise was insistent. During a heated argument over why Jim always left the garage a mess, he finally gave Elise an ultimatum: she had to see a psychiatrist, or he was moving out.

Elise's internist referred her to a psychiatrist and at her first appointment, Elise announced that she was only there to please her husband and didn't really think she had a problem. After all, if Jim would just start picking up after himself, everything would be fine.

As she continued to talk, Elise revealed some of her unresolved issues about pleasing her mother and remaining in control of her life. She also admitted to feeling unbearable anxiety if something was messy or out of place, and she couldn't stop herself from straightening things out.

*   *   *

Elise suffered from obsessive-compulsive disorder or OCD. This condition, compounded with her mother's upcoming visit, was escalating her need for tidiness. It became clear that Jim was not the problem—it was Elise's deep-rooted need to be in control of every aspect of her life, especially her immediate environment.

Obsessive-compulsive disorder is a form of anxiety involving unwanted and repeated thoughts and feelings (obsessions) and the urge to engage in behaviors (compulsions) in response to these obsessions. It afflicts approximately 2 percent of the general population. The condition can become quite debilitating, disrupting nearly all aspects of a person's ability to function in life. Less severe forms of the symptoms are relatively common—a large US survey indicated that more than one-quarter of people report experiencing obsessions or compulsions at some point during their lives.

The underlying cause of OCD is not known, but both environmental and genetic factors are thought to play a role. Brain imaging studies show abnormal neural activity in the frontal and temporal brain regions during symptom provocation. Some areas of the grey matter—the outer rim of the brain—show increased volumes in patients with OCD. Studies of brain neurotransmitters indicate changes in the serotonin and dopamine systems associated with the condition. Serotonin deficits have also been associated with depressive illnesses, and dopamine is involved in the brain's reward and pleasure circuits.

DO YOU HAVE OCD SYMPTOMS?

To get an idea of whether you have obsessive-compulsive tendencies, check off as many of the following experiences that apply to you:

☐   unwanted impulses, ideas, or images

☐   excessive worry about dirt, germs, or toxins

☐   fear that you will lose something important

☐   constant worry that something bad will happen because you forgot to lock the door, turn off an appliance, etc.

☐   urge to constantly do things to reduce your anxiety

☐   washing yourself or things around you excessively

☐   urge to incessantly check things or repeat actions to make sure they are done right

☐   need to keep useless items because you can't throw them away

If you checked off four or more of the above, you may be suffering from symptoms of OCD.

CHARACTERISTIC FEATURES
AND DIAGNOSIS OF OCD

Because medical conditions can cause symptoms of OCD, a physical examination and laboratory tests to rule out thyroid, metabolic, or other physical abnormalities are often indicated. To determine the presence of obsessions and compulsions and whether someone meets the diagnostic criteria for OCD, mental health professionals may use a standardized rating scale, such as the Yale-Brown Obsessive-Compulsive Scale (Y-BOCS).

The obsessions can take the form of fears of contamination or unwanted aggressive thoughts, and the compulsions often involve excessive cleaning, handwashing, or ordering or rearranging things. The symptoms can change over time and often worsen as a result of psychological stress.

Symptoms of OCD usually begin before age thirty-five, and the average age of onset is approximately twenty years old. Usually symptoms start gradually, and if left untreated, the condition becomes chronic. However, symptoms tend to wax and wane depending on the patient's current situation and stress levels.

OCD AND YOUR BRAIN

University of Cambridge neuroscientists performed functional MRI scanning to measure brain activity in patients with OCD. They found that patients and their close relatives showed low activity levels in brain regions controlling a person's ability to stop habitual behaviors. Even though it's known that OCD runs in families, the precise genetics are uncertain.

Other research using positron emission tomography (PET) scanning has shown that both psychotherapy and antidepressant treatment alter brain neural function. Many of these studies have focused on the cingulate cortex, a brain region involved with emotional processing, learning, and memory. Treatment has been shown to decrease metabolism in this brain region, and the level of decrease in regional brain metabolism is associated with the degree of symptom relief.

Children who have suffered physical or sexual abuse or other early life stressors have an increased risk of developing OCD. Someone with a family history of a parent or sibling with OCD has a twofold greater risk of developing the disorder than those without such a family history.

Although males and females have relatively similar risks for developing OCD, symptoms can vary according to gender. Women with OCD are more likely to experience symptoms related to cleaning, as was the case for Elise. On the other hand, men have a greater likelihood of experiencing symptoms of forbidden thoughts or concerns about asymmetry.

OCD SYMPTOM THEMES

Each individual with OCD experiences a different constellation of obsessions and compulsions. However, the symptoms take on particular themes or dimensions.

Theme	Symptoms
Cleaning	Contamination obsessions and cleaning compulsions
Symmetry	Obsessions about symmetry and repeating, ordering, and counting compulsions
Forbidden or taboo thoughts	Aggressive, sexual, and religious obsessions and compulsions
Harm	Fears of harming oneself or others
Discarding and accumulating	Hoarding objects

People with OCD experience tremendous distress—approximately 50 percent of them report suicidal thinking, and one out of four has attempted suicide. Patients with OCD also try to ignore or suppress their obsessions and compulsions, which does not reduce their levels of anxiety. Although compulsions are not pleasurable experiences, some people report feeling reduced anxiety after carrying out the compulsive behaviors.

DIAGNOSTIC FEATURES OF OCD

Specific diagnostic criteria have been described in the American Psychiatric Association's Diagnostic and Statistical Manual of Mental Disorders and include the following features:

- There is a presence of obsessions, compulsions, or both.

- The obsessions or compulsions are time-consuming, cause significant distress, or impair normal functioning.

- The obsessive-compulsive symptoms are not attributable to the physiological effects of another illness or substance abuse and are not explained by another mental disorder.

Those who suffer from OCD often avoid people, places, things, and situations that trigger their obsessions and compulsions. For example, someone who obsesses about contamination would likely avoid restaurants and public restrooms. Patients who worry about harming themselves would likely avoid razor blades, cliffs, or ledges.

OTHER OCD-RELATED DISORDERS

In the American Psychiatric Association's Diagnostic and Statistical Manual of Mental Disorders, OCD is categorized apart from other anxiety disorders, although it certainly results in tremendous anxiety for the sufferer. The following are other related disorders included in the obsessive-compulsive category:

Disorder	Description
Body dysmorphic disorder	Preoccupation with one or more perceived flaws in one's physical appearance that are not observable to others
Hoarding disorder	Persistent difficulty discarding or parting with possessions regardless of their actual value
Trichotillomania	Recurrent pulling out of one's hair, resulting in hair loss and sometimes baldness
Excoriation disorder	Recurrent skin picking resulting in skin lesions
Obsessional jealousy	Nondelusional preoccupation with a partner's perceived infidelity

These symptoms clearly disrupt people's lives. Incessant checking of door locks and stoves left on can make it impossible for a person to leave home. Compulsive handwashing can lead to dermatological conditions. Many OCD symptoms can have a major impact on relationships—Elise's cleanliness led to her husband's threat to leave her. OCD patients may attempt to impose rules and prohibitions on others in their lives, which often causes considerable distress to close friends and family members.

TREATMENT OF OCD

Treatments for OCD have been shown to help bring symptoms under control so that they do not disrupt the patient's ability to function in life. Because of the chronic nature of the condition, some patients require treatment for the rest of their lives. Both psychotherapy and medications are effective and have their best effect when used in combination.

Cognitive behavioral therapy (CBT) is effective for many OCD patients and involves exposing patients gradually to the feared object or obsession. For example, for patients obsessed with cleanliness, the therapist first helps them feel comfortable just looking at dirt. Once they overcome that fear, the therapist then helps them cope with their anxiety associated with actually touching dirt, and so forth. For patients who are too anxious about even looking at or touching real dirt, the therapist might use imaginal exposure or visualization. With this approach, the therapist helps the patient imagine the dirt while controlling their anxiety symptoms. As patients become more comfortable with the anxiety associated with visualizing dirt, they are gradually desensitized to the feared situation, which makes it easier to move on to real-life exposure of the feared substance.

DID YOU KNOW?

- *Koro* is a culture-specific syndrome wherein sufferers experience intense anxiety as they obsess about their genitalia receding into their body and possibly causing death.

- Few OCD patients respond to placebos, while anywhere from 30 to 40 percent of depressed patients experience a placebo response.

Several medicines have been shown to be effective in helping control both the obsessions and compulsions of OCD. The first line of pharmacotherapy is an antidepressant. The Food and Drug Administration

(FDA) has approved all the following antidepressant medications for the treatment of OCD: clomipramine (Anafranil), fluoxetine (Prozac), fluvoxamine (Luvox), paroxetine (Paxil), and sertraline (Zoloft).

Although Elise initially became defensive when her psychiatrist explained her condition, eventually, she was willing to give medication a try. She also gradually got over her defensiveness and agreed to engage in weekly psychotherapy with a psychologist who specialized in CBT. The therapist had Elise develop a symptom list in order of severity and helped her with exposure therapy. During these sessions, they used Elise's symptom list and systematically exposed Elise to her fears. They started with the least anxiety-provoking ones on the list and gradually increased her tolerance for things being messy or disordered. The therapist also helped Elise get a better perspective on her symptom triggers, such as her mother's visit, spring cleaning, and marital stress.

Elise continued to be a nitpicker over the years, but her medication and therapy reduced her OCD symptoms considerably. Elise still became tense when her mother visited, but her treatment dramatically improved her relationship with Jim.

A healthy lifestyle including proper nutrition, regular exercise, restful sleep, and relaxation strategies can help reduce symptoms of OCD as it does with other disorders associated with anxiety. Research on new and innovative interventions is ongoing. Some patients with OCD or any anxiety disorder have tried St. John's wort, but placebo-controlled trials have not confirmed its efficacy. Repetitive transcranial magnetic stimulation, or rTMS, is a relatively noninvasive treatment that involves placing a small, neural-stimulating device directly on the skull and has been used to reduce symptoms. Deep brain stimulation and even brain surgery have been used to treat severe OCD symptoms.

Epilogue

WHETHER YOU EXPERIENCE MILD anxiety symptoms from time to time or an actual anxiety disorder, the information in this guide has hopefully helped you better understand your symptoms and ways to effectively deal with them. In addition to the major anxiety disorders discussed, people suffering from a variety of other psychiatric conditions also experience anxiety symptoms. For example, individuals experiencing symptoms of trauma and stressor-related disorders, such as posttraumatic stress disorder or adjustment disorder, certainly suffer from symptoms of anxiety. Moreover, anxiety symptoms can be prominent in depressive disorders, eating disorders, and many other major psychiatric disorders. If you are concerned about any mental symptoms that you or a loved one are experiencing, talking with your doctor or mental health professional is an important first step to getting help.

Many other resources are available in the community to help people cope with anxiety symptoms and disorders. Organizations such as the Anxiety and Depression Association of America (www.adaa .org), the American Psychiatric Association (www .psychiatry.org), the American Psychological Association (www.apa.org), and the National Institute of Mental Health (www.nimh.nih.gov) have websites with information about these conditions and strategies for getting help and referrals. The good news is that most forms of anxiety do respond to treatment once accurately diagnosed. The sooner you get help, the sooner you can enjoy your life without the hindrance of the sometimes annoying and other times debilitating symptoms of anxiety.

Bibliography

PROLOGUE

Bandelow, B., and Michaelis, S. "Epidemiology of Anxiety Disorders in the 21st Century." *Dialogues Clin Neurosci* 17 (2015): 327–35.

CHAPTER 1: WHAT IS ANXIETY?

American College Health Association. *American College Health Association-National College Health Assessment II: Undergraduate Student Reference Group Executive Summary Fall 2016.* Hanover, MD: American College Health Association, 2017.

American Psychiatric Association. *Diagnostic and Statistical Manual of Mental Disorders* (5th ed.). Arlington, VA: American Psychiatric Publishing; 2013.

Coplan, J. D., et al. "The Relationship between Intel-
    ligence and Anxiety: An Association with Sub-
    cortical White Matter Metabolism." *Front Evol
    Neurosci* 3, no. 8 (2011). https://doiorg/10.3389/
    fnevo.2011.00008.
Huffman, J. C., et al. "Panic Disorder and Chest Pain:
    Mechanisms, Morbidity, and Management." *Prim
    Care Companion J Clin Psychiatry* 4 (2002): 54–62.
Jacka, F. N., et al. "Association of Western and Tra-
    ditional Diets with Depression and Anxiety in
    Women." *Am J Psychiatry* 167 (2010): 305–11.
Katerndahl, D. A. "Chest Pain and Its Importance in
    Patients with Panic Disorder: An Updated Litera-
    ture Review." *Prim Care Companion J Clin Psychi-
    atry* 10 (2008): 376–83.
Krusemark, E. A., and Li, W. "Enhanced Olfactory
    Sensory Perception of Threat in Anxiety: An
    Event-Related fMRI Study." *Chemosensory Percep-
    tion* 5 (2012): 37–45.
Llewellyn, N., et al. "Reframing Thoughts to Reduce
    Anxiety: Reappraisal and Suppression Mediate
    the Contribution of Regulatory Focus to Anxiety
    in Healthy Adults." *Emotion* 13 (2013): 610–15.
National Institute of Mental Health. https://www
    .nimh.nih.gov/health/statistics/.
Penney, A. M., et al. "Intelligence and Emotional Dis-
    orders: Is the Worrying and Ruminating Mind a
    More Intelligent Mind?" *Personality and Individ-
    ual Differences* 74 (2015): 90–93.

Schonfeld, W. H., et al. "The Functioning and Well-Being of Patients with Unrecognized Anxiety Disorders and Major Depressive Disorder." *J Affective Disorders* 43 (1997): 105–19.

CHAPTER 2: DO-IT-YOURSELF STRATEGIES FOR REDUCING ANXIETY

Andersson, G., et al. "The Use of the Internet in the Treatment of Anxiety Disorders." *Curr Opin Psychiatry* 18 (2005): 73–77.

Broocks, A., et al. "Comparison of Aerobic Exercise, Clomipramine, and Placebo in the Treatment of Panic Disorder." *Am J Psychiatry* 155 (1998): 603–9.

Desai, R., et al. "Effects of Yoga on Brain Waves and Structural Activation: A Review." *Complement Ther Clin Pract* 21 (2015): 112–18.

Fiona, S., et al. "International Tables of Glycemic Index and Glycemic Load Values." *Diabetes Care* 31 (2008): 2281–83.

Harvard Health Publications; Harvard Medical School. *Harvard Heart Letter*, March 17, 2017. http://www.health.harvard.edu/diet-and-weight-loss/calories-burned-in-30-minutes-of-leisure-and-routine-activities.

Hirai, M., and Clum, G. A. "A Meta-analytic Study of Self-Help Interventions for Anxiety Problems." *Behav Ther* 37 (2006): 99–111.

Hudson, C., et al. "Protein-Source Tryptophan as an Efficacious Treatment for Social Anxiety Disorder: A Pilot Study." *Can J Physiol Pharmacol* 85 (2007): 928–32.

Jacka, F. N, et al. "Association of Western and Traditional Diets with Depression and Anxiety in Women." *Am J Psychiatry* 167 (2010): 305–11.

Jorm, A. F., Christensen, H., Griffiths, K. M., Parslow, R. A., Rodgers, B., and Blewitt, K. A. "Effectiveness of Complementary and Self-Help Treatments for Anxiety Disorders." Supplement, *Med J Aust* 181, no. S7 (2004): S29–S46.

Kirkwood, G., et al. "Yoga for Anxiety: A Systematic Review of the Research Evidence." *Br J Sports Med* 39 (2005): 884–91.

Koszycki, D, et al. "Randomized Trial of a Meditation-Based Stress Reduction Program and Cognitive Behavior Therapy in Generalized Social Anxiety Disorder." *Behav Res Ther* 45 (2007): 2518–26.

Last, N., et al. "The Effects of Meditation on Grey Matter Atrophy and Neurodegeneration: A Systematic Review." *J Alzheimers Dis* 56 (2017): 275–86.

Lee, S. H., et al. "Effectiveness of a Meditation-Based Stress Management Program as an Adjunct to Pharmacotherapy in Patients with Anxiety Disorder." *J Psychosom Res* 62 (2007): 189–95.

Low Dog, T. "The Role of Nutrition in Mental Health." *Altern Ther Health Med* 16 (2010): 42–46.

National Institute for Health and Clinical Excellence. *Computerised Cognitive Behaviour Therapy for Depression and Anxiety.* Review of Technology Appraisal 51. London: NICE, 2006.

Seabrook, E. M., et al. "Social Networking Sites, Depression, and Anxiety: A Systematic Review." *JMIR Ment Health* 3, no. 4 (2016): e50.

Tumur, I., et al. "Computerised Cognitive Behaviour Therapy for Obsessive-Compulsive Disorder: A Systematic Review." *Psychother Psychosom* 76 (2007): 196–202.

Wipfli, B. M., et al. "The Anxiolytic Effects of Exercise: A Meta-analysis of Randomized Trials and Dose-Response Analysis." *J Sport Exerc Psychol* 30 (2008): 392–410.

CHAPTER 3: CONVENTIONAL
TREATMENTS THAT WORK

Antony, M. M., and Stein, M. B. *Oxford Handbook of Anxiety and Related Disorders.* Oxford: Oxford University Press, 2008.

A-Tiak, J. G., et al. "A Meta-analysis of the Efficacy of Acceptance and Commitment Therapy for Clinically Relevant Mental and Physical Health Problems." *Psychother Psychosom* 84 (2015): 30–36. https://doi.org/10.1159/000365764. Epub ahead of print, Dec. 24, 2014.

Bystritsky, A., et al. "Current Diagnosis and Treatment of Anxiety Disorders." *Pharmacy and Therapeutics* 38 (2013): 41–44.

Fredette, C., et al. "Using Hypnosis in the Treatment of Anxiety Disorders: Pros and Cons." In *New Insights into Anxiety Disorders*, edited by F. Durbano, 343–77. InTech, 2013. ISBN 978-953-51-1053-8. https://doi.org/10.5772/46003.

Hofmann, S. G., et al. "The Efficacy of Cognitive Behavioral Therapy: A Review of Meta-analyses." *Cognitive Therapy and Research* 36 (2012): 427–40.

Hofmann, S. T., et al. "The Effect of Mindfulness-Based Therapy on Anxiety and Depression: A Meta-analytic Review." *J Consult Clin Psychol* 78 (2010): 169–83.

Swedish Council on Health Technology Assessment. *Treatment of Anxiety Disorders: A Systematic Review*. SBU Yellow Report No. 171/1+2, November 2005.

Thomaes, K., et al. "Degrading Traumatic Memories with Eye Movements: A Pilot Functional MRI Study in PTSD." *Eur J Psychotraumatol* 7 (Nov. 29, 2016): 31371. https://doi.org/10.3402/ejpt.v7.31371. eCollection 2016.

CHAPTER 4: ALTERNATIVE THERAPIES

Davidson, J. R., et al. "Homeopathic Treatments in Psychiatry: A Systematic Review of Randomized Placebo-Controlled Studies." *J Clin Psychiatry* 72 (2011): 795–805.

D'Urso, G., et al. "Transcranial Direct Current Stimulation for Obsessive-Compulsive Disorder: A Randomized, Controlled, Partial Cover Trial." *Depress Anxiety* 33 (2016): 1132–40.

Fedotova, J., et al. "Therapeutical Strategies for Anxiety and Anxiety-like Disorders Using Plant-Derived Natural Compounds and Plant Extracts." *Biomed Pharmacother* 95 (2017): 437–46.

Field, T. "Massage Therapy Research Review." *Complement Ther Clin Pract* 20 (2014): 224–29.

Iannone, A. "Transcranial Magnetic Stimulation and Transcranial Direct Current Stimulation Appear to Be Safe Neuromodulatory Techniques Useful in the Treatment of Anxiety Disorders and Other Neuropsychiatric Disorders." *Arq Neuropsiquiatr* 74 (2016): 829–35.

Joyce, J., and Herbison, G. P. "Reiki for Depression and Anxiety." *Cochrane Database Syst Rev* 4 (Apr. 3, 2015): CD006833. https://doi.org/10.1002/14651858.CD006833.pub2.

Kessler, R. C., et al. "The Use of Complementary and Alternative Therapies to Treat Anxiety and

Depression in the United States." *Am J Psychiatry* 158 (2001): 289–94.

Lakhan, S. E., and Vieira, K. F. "Nutritional and Herbal Supplements for Anxiety and Anxiety-Related Disorders: Systematic Review." *Nutrition Journal* 9 (2010): 42. http://www.nutritionj.com/content/9/1/42.

Lebowitz, K. R., et al. "Effects of Humor and Laughter on Psychological Functioning, Quality of Life, Health Status, and Pulmonary Functioning among Patients with Chronic Obstructive Pulmonary Disease: A Preliminary Investigation." *Heart Lung* 40 (2011): 310–19.

Marzbani, H., et al. "Neurofeedback: A Comprehensive Review on System Design, Methodology and Clinical Applications." *Basic Clin Neurosci* 7 (2016): 143–58.

Mizrachi Zer-Aviv, T., et al. "Cannabinoids and Posttraumatic Stress Disorder: Clinical and Preclinical Evidence for Treatment and Prevention." *Behav Pharmacol* 27 (2016): 561–69.

Pilkington, K. "Acupuncture Therapy for Psychiatric Illness." *Int Rev Neurobiol* 111 (2013): 197–216.

Saeed, S. A., Bloch, R. M., and Antonacci, D. J. "Herbal and Dietary Supplements for Treatment of Anxiety Disorders." *American Family Physician* 76 (2007): 549–56.

Shin, E. S., et al. "Massage with or without Aromatherapy for Symptom Relief in People with Cancer." *Cochrane*

Database Syst Rev 6 (June 3, 2016): CD009873.
https://doi.org/10.1002/14651858.CD009873.pub3.

Soares, V. P., and Campos, A. C. "Evidences for the
Anti-panic Actions of Cannabidiol." *Curr Neuro-
pharmacol* 15 (2017): 291–99.

CHAPTER 5: WORRIED SICK:
GENERALIZED ANXIETY DISORDER

American Psychiatric Association. *Diagnostic and
Statistical Manual of Mental Disorders.* 5th ed.
Arlington, VA: American Psychiatric Publishing,
2013.

Antony, M. M., and Stein, M. B. *Oxford Handbook of
Anxiety and Related Disorders.* Oxford: Oxford
University Press, 2008.

Bystritsky, A., et al. "Current Diagnosis and Treatment
of Anxiety Disorders." *Pharmacy and Therapeutics*
38 (2013): 41–44.

Newman, M. G., et al. "Worry and Generalized Anxiety Disorder: A Review and Theoretical Synthesis
of Evidence on Nature, Etiology, Mechanisms, and
Treatment." *Annual Review of Clinical Psychology*
9 (2013): 275–97.

CHAPTER 6: GRIPPED BY FEAR: PANIC DISORDER

American Psychiatric Association. *Diagnostic and Statistical Manual of Mental Disorders*. 5th ed. Arlington, VA: American Psychiatric Publishing, 2013.

Batelaan, N. M., et al. "Evidence-Based Pharmacotherapy of Panic Disorder: An Update." *International Journal of Neuropsychopharmacology* 15 (2012): 403–15.

Caldirola, D., et al. "Personalized Medicine in Panic Disorder: Where Are We Now? A Meta-regression Analysis." *Personalized Medicine in Psychiatry* 1–2 (2017): 26. https://doi.org/10.1016/j.pmip.2016.12.003.

Kessler, R. C., et al. "The Epidemiology of Panic Attacks, Panic Disorder, and Agoraphobia in the National Comorbidity Survey Replication." *Arch Gen Psychiatry* 63 (2006): 415–24.

Taylor, C. B. "Panic Disorder." *British Medical Journal* 332 (2006): 951–55.

CHAPTER 7: SHY TO A FAULT: SOCIAL ANXIETY

Acarturk, C., et al. "Psychological Treatment of Social Anxiety Disorder: A Meta-analysis." *Psychological Medicine* 39 (2009): 241–54.

Addolorato, G., et al. "Anxiety and Depression: A Common Feature of Health Care Seeking Patients with Irritable Bowel Syndrome and Food Allergy." *Hepatogastroenterology* 45 (1998): 1559–64.

American Psychiatric Association. *Diagnostic and Statistical Manual of Mental Disorders*. 5th ed. Arlington, VA: American Psychiatric Publishing, 2013.

Boraxbekk, C. J., et al. "Neuroplasticity in Response to Cognitive Behavior Therapy for Social Anxiety Disorder." *Translational Psychiatry* 6 (Feb. 2016). https://doi.org/10.1038/tp.2015.218.

Furmark, T., et al. "Common Changes in Cerebral Blood Flow in Patients with Social Phobia Treated with Citalopram or Cognitive-Behavioral Therapy." *Arch Gen Psychiatry* 59 (2002): 425–33.

Goodwin, R. D. "Association between Physical Activity and Mental Disorders among Adults in the United States." *Prev Med* 36 (2003): 698–703.

Jacka, F. N., et al. "Association of Western and Traditional Diets with Depression and Anxiety in Women." *Am J Psychiatry* 167 (2010): 305–11.

Jacka, F. N., et al. "The Association between Habitual Diet Quality and the Common Mental Disorders in Community-Dwelling Adults: The Hordaland Health Study." *Psychosom Med* 73 (2011): 483–90.

Jayakody, K., et al. "Exercise for Anxiety Disorders: Systematic Review." *Br J Sports Med* 43 (2014): 187–96.

Kushnir, J., et al. "The Link between Social Anxiety Disorder, Treatment Outcome, and Sleep Difficulties among Patients Receiving Cognitive Behavioural Group Therapy." *Sleep Med* 15 (2014): 515–21.

Nordahl, H. M., et al. "Paroxetine, Cognitive Therapy or Their Combination in the Treatment of Social Anxiety Disorder with and without Avoidant Personality Disorder: A Randomized Clinical Trial." *Psychother Psychosom* 85, no. 6 (2016): 346. https://doi.org/10.1159/000447013.

Ossman, W. A., Wilson, K. G., Storaasli, R. D., and McNeill, J. W. "A Preliminary Investigation of the Use of Acceptance and Commitment Therapy in Group Treatment for Social Phobia." *Rev Int Psicol Ter Psicol* 6 (2006): 397–416.

Powers, M., et al. "A Meta-analytic Review of Psychological Treatments for Social Anxiety Disorder." *International Journal of Cognitive Therapy* 1 (2008): 94–113.

Roy-Byrne, P. P., et al. "Pharmacological Treatments for Panic Disorder, Generalized Anxiety Disorder, Specific Phobia, and Social Anxiety Disorder." In *A Guide to Treatments That Work*, 3rd ed., edited by P. E. Nathan and J. M. Gorman, 395–430. New York: Oxford University Press, 2007.

Zalta, A. K., et al. "Sleep Quality Predicts Treatment Outcome in CBT for Social Anxiety Disorder." *Depress Anxiety* 30 (2013): 1114–20.

CHAPTER 8: GERMS, BUGS, AND
HEIGHTS, OH MY: PHOBIAS

American Psychiatric Association. *Diagnostic and Statistical Manual of Mental Disorders*. 5th ed. Arlington, VA: American Psychiatric Publishing, 2013.

Costa, R. T. D., et al. "Virtual Reality Exposure Therapy for Fear of Driving: Analysis of Clinical Characteristics, Physiological Response, and Sense of Presence." *Rev Bras Psiquiatr* (Feb. 15, 2018). https://doi.org/10.1590/1516-4446-2017-2270. Epub ahead of print.

Gujjar, K. R., et al. "Virtual Reality Exposure Therapy for Treatment of Dental Phobia." *Dent Update* 44 (2017): 423–24, 427–28, 431–32, 435.

Kessler, R. C., et al. "Lifetime Prevalence and Age-of-Onset Distributions of DSM-IV Disorders in the National Comorbidity Survey Replication (NCS-R)." *Arch Gen Psychiatry* 62 (2005): 593–602.

Linares, I. M. P., et al. "Neuroimaging in Specific Phobia Disorder: A Systematic Review of the Literature." *Rev Bras Psiquiatr* 34 (2012): 101–11.

Öst, L. G. "One-Session Treatment for Specific Phobias." *Behaviour Research and Therapy* 27 (1989): 1–7.

Sarris, J., et al. "Complementary Medicine, Exercise, Meditation, Diet, and Lifestyle Modification for Anxiety Disorders: A Review of Current

Evidence." *Evid Based-Complement Alternat Med*
2012 (2012): 809653. https://doi.org/10.1155/2012/
809653.

Wolitzky-Taylor, K. B., et al. "Psychological Approaches
in the Treatment of Specific Phobias: A Meta-
analysis." *Clinical Psychology Review* 28 (2008):
1021–37.

CHAPTER 9: CAN'T STOP THOSE THOUGHTS: OBSESSIVE-COMPULSIVE DISORDER

American Psychiatric Association. *Diagnostic and
Statistical Manual of Mental Disorders.* 5th ed.
Arlington, VA: American Psychiatric Publishing,
2013.

Chamberlain, S. R., et al. "Orbitofrontal Dysfunction
in Patients with Obsessive-Compulsive Disorder and Their Unaffected Relatives." *Science* 321
(2008): 421–22.

Fineberg, N. A., et al. "Evidence-Based Pharmacotherapy of Obsessive-Compulsive Disorder." *Intl J
Neuropsychopharm* 15 (2012): 1173–91.

Goodman, W. K., et al. "The Yale-Brown Obsessive
Compulsive Scale (Y-BOCS): Part 1. Development, Use and Reliability." *Arch Gen Psychiatry* 46
(1989): 1006–11.

Kobak, K. A., et al. "St John's Wort versus Placebo in
Obsessive-Compulsive Disorder: Results from a

Double-Blind Study." *Int Clin Psychopharmacol* 20 (2005): 299–304.

Lack, C. W. "Obsessive-Compulsive Disorder: Evidence-Based Treatments and Future Directions for Research." *World J Psychiatry* 2 (2012): 86–90.

Pepper, J., et al. "Deep Brain Stimulation versus Anterior Capsulotomy for Obsessive-Compulsive Disorder: A Review of the Literature." *J Neurosurg* 122 (2015): 1028–37.

Perani, D., et al. "[18F]FDG PET Study in Obsessive-Compulsive Disorder: A Clinical/Metabolic Correlation Study after Treatment." *Br J Psychiatry* 166 (1995): 244–50.

Ravindran, A. V., and da Silva, T. L. "Complementary and Alternative Therapies as Add-on to Pharmacotherapy for Mood and Anxiety Disorders: A Systematic Review." *J Affect Disord* 150 (2013): 707–19.

Sugarman, M. A., et al. "Obsessive-Compulsive Disorder Has a Reduced Placebo (and Antidepressant) Response Compared to Other Anxiety Disorders: A Meta-analysis." *J Affect Disord* 218 (2017): 217–26.

Index

Page numbers followed by *f* and *t* refer to figures and tables, respectively.

About the Authors

GARY SMALL, M.D., and GIGI VORGAN are the authors of *The New York Times* bestseller *The Memory Bible*, as well as *The Memory Prescription*, *The Longevity Bible*, *iBrain*, *The Other Side of the Couch*, *The Alzheimer's Prevention Program*, *2 Weeks to a Younger Brain*, and *SNAP!*. Dr. Small is a Professor of Psychiatry and Biobehavioral Sciences and Director of the Longevity Center at the Semel Institute for Neuroscience & Human Behavior at the University of California, Los Angeles. Named one of the world's leading innovators in science and technology by *Scientific American*, he has appeared frequently on *Today*, *Good Morning America*, PBS, and CNN and lectures throughout the world. Ms. Vorgan, in addition to working as a coauthor with her husband Dr. Small, has written feature films and television. She and Dr. Small live together in Los Angeles.

For more information on their books and Dr. Small's appearances, visit www.DrGarySmall.com.

RateMyMemory
Powered by newsmax❤health

Normal Forgetfulness?
Something More Serious?

You forget things — names of people, where you parked your car, the place you put an important document, and so much more. Some experts tell you to dismiss these episodes.

"Not so fast," says Dr. Gary Small, director of the UCLA Longevity Center, medical researcher, professor of psychiatry, and the *New York Times* best-selling author of *2 Weeks to a Younger Brain.*

Dr. Small says that most age-related memory issues are normal but sometimes can be a warning sign of future cognitive decline.

Now Dr. Small has created the online **RateMyMemory Test** — allowing you to easily assess your memory strength in just a matter of minutes.

It's time to begin your journey of making sure your brain stays healthy and young! **It takes just 2 minutes!**

Test Your Memory Today:
MemoryRate.com/Anxiety